Planni

New Career

How to take stock, change course, and secure a better future for yourself

JUDITH JOHNSTONE
3rd edition

How To Books

By the same author
Applying for a Job
Passing That Interview

Acknowledgements
My grateful thanks to the many members of the British Psychological Society who provided basic information for the original edition of this book; staff of the Open University,
Benefits Agency, DfEE, Barclays Bank and NatWest for leaflets and advice on financial
matters; Cumbria Careers – particularly George Neal for details on national services for
adults; and John Flaherty of Cumbria Enterprise on the changes to the Training Access
Points provision and local initiatives.

Special thanks must go to George Summerfield, who during his time as Consultant
Director of Career Analysts readily agreed to making available the case studies, and particularly to Alexis Hallam, Consultant Psychologist, for her patience and time in research-
ing my requirements so diligently. All the names mentioned in the case studies are pseu-
donyms, with the exception of Simon Capp, who featured in an article in The *Times* on the
subject of making a career out of a hobby.

Published by
How To Books Ltd, 3 Newtec Place,
Magdalen Road, Oxford OX4 1RE, United Kingdom
Tel: (01865) 793806   Fax: (01865) 248780

Third edition (revised and updated) 1999

British Library Cataloguing in Publication Data
A catalogue record for this book is available from
the British Library

Editing by Diana Brueton / Cartoons by Mike Flanagan
Cover design by Shireen Nathoo Design
Cover image PhotoDisc

Produced for How To Books by Deer Park Productions
Typeset by Concept Communications Ltd, Crayford, Kent
Printed and bound by Cromwell Press, Trowbridge, Wiltshire

NOTE: The material contained in this book is set out in good
faith for general guidance and no liability can be accepted
for loss or expense incurred as a result of relying in particular
circumstances on statements made in the book. The laws and
regulations are complex and liable to change, and readers should
check the current position with the relevant authorities before
making personal arrangements.

How To Books

Planning a
New Career

How To Books are designed to help people achieve their goals. They are for everyone wishing to acquire new skills, develop self-reliance, or change their lives for the better. They are accessible, easy to read and easy to act on. Other titles in the series include:

Applying for a Job
How to sell your skills and experience to a prospective employer

Passing that Interview
Your step-by-step guide to achieving success

Enhancing your Employability
How to improve your prospects of achieving a fulfilling and rewarding career

Finding a Job with a Future
How to identify and work in growth industries and services

Getting That Job
The complete job finders handbook

Writing a CV that Works
How to develop and use your key marketing tool

The *How To Series* now contains around 200 titles in the following categories:

Business & Management
Computer Basics
General Reference
Jobs & Careers
Living & Working Abroad
Personal Finance
Self-Development
Small Business
Student Handbooks
Successful Writing

For full details, please send to our distributors for a free copy of the latest catalogue:

How To Books
Customer Services Dept.
Plymbridge Distributors Ltd, Estover Road
Plymouth PL6 7PZ, United Kingdom
Tel: 01752 202301   Fax: 01752 202331
http://www.howtobooks.co.uk

Contents

List of Illustrations

Preface

to the Third Edition

There are very few careers in today's working environment which can safely be thought of as being 'for life'. Shifts in world trade, competition from Third World countries, the decline of manufacturing and tradition- al industries in the UK, and the rise of the service sector have already made an impact on the range of careers and jobs available. The unknown quantities of the emerging East European economies and the effects of closer integration within the European Union will impact further in the future. Other factors are also playing their part: the rapid expansion of technology into almost every workplace; the increased emphasis on value for money, demands for greater productivity, and the need for a more flexible, multi-skilled workforce.

Gone are the old certainties. Organisations and businesses have been forced to restructure and reshape to survive. Whole layers of manage- ment and large numbers of ordinary run-of-the-mill jobs have disap- peared. Short-term contracts, part-time working, job-sharing, home- working, annual hours and a range of other formats are increasingly replacing the rigid structures of yesteryear. Change is everywhere and shows no sign of slowing down. Hundreds of thousands of people are having to rethink their working lives. For those just starting out there is the likelihood of facing not just one, but possibly two career changes before they retire.

Changing direction can be like taking a leap into the dark: perilous and often frightening.

On the one hand you can be forced into the situation by cutbacks in staffing levels or the closure of a business, whether this is your own or someone else's. Alternatively, you may take the initiative yourself to make the break from a job which has ceased to have any real meaning for you. Either way, you are almost certain to feel anxious about the future.

Whatever reason lies behind your change in circumstances however, whether you feel down, or elated by the prospect that lies before you, you have an unparalleled opportunity to wipe the slate clean and start again. For that reason alone you should give yourself a little space and time to take stock of your personal situation in detail and to get to know yourself better. If you do this, then you can start out on the road to your new career far more confident that you are heading in the right direction.

This book is to help you plan your voyage of self-discovery. It looks at who you are; what you are; what made you the way you are, and where you want to go to from here. It helps you evaluate your life skills both inside and outside the workplace; to put your personal circumstances into perspective; to recognise for yourself which careers you should concentrate on to suit you best; where to seek help if needed; how not to make the same mistakes again — if you made any before — and how to be realistic about what you ultimately want to achieve.

Providing you are well prepared, changing direction is not as daunting as it first appears: it can be exciting and challenging, offering you the golden opportunity of a new beginning.

Judith Johnstone

1

Moving On

REVIEWING YOUR SITUATION

The purpose of this chapter is to set you thinking about the reasons why you are searching for a new career; what if anything can be learnt from these, and what you need to know about yourself before embarking on any new venture. This process should not be rushed. STOP and THINK. Allow yourself the mental space necessary to make the right decisions and to lay solid foundations for a sound plan of action.

Your main difficulty at this time is likely to be the pressure on you to 'do something'. Your family and financial commitments may be so great that worry leaves you little room for careful reflection or sound planning.

In the first flush of anxiety to get back into the jobs market, there is always the temptation to throw yourself at every available opening on offer, irrespective of whether it is suitable or not. This 'scatter-gun' approach to the job search can be totally counter-productive. How many times do you hear stories about people who send out hundreds of job applications but never make it to the shortlist? Their lack of success is often quoted to illustrate how bad the jobs market is, or how impossible it is to get employment even with experience and good qualifications. But the real lesson to be learnt is that ill-thought out or rushed applications lead nowhere. No employer (or financial backer if you are hoping to set up in business) is going to give you a second glance if you are clearly unsuitable for the job. Don't sell yourself short.

To succeed, you have to target your new job precisely. To do this you must be confident you know where you are going, and why. The answers to these questions are unique to you, and the clues to help you unravel the mystery lie buried somewhere in your own personal history and the make-up of who you are.

HOW DID I GET HERE?

The world of work has changed dramatically in the last decade. The workplace has altered out of all recognition. Computers are now the norm, not the exception. Communication is no longer limited to letters, telephones and fax machines. In the UK, the impact of the Internet is only just beginning. Computer literacy is now a prime skill. There are few openings for those without it.

Organisational structures have also changed. Whole layers of management have been cut away. Multi-skilling is what is required of everyone. Flexibility is the name of the game. If you have only one string to your bow, your chances of employment are limited.

In the wider world, what happens to the global economy has a knock-on effect closer to home. The collapse of confidence in a currency in the Far East can have unexpected consequences for the UK economy. Even successful businesses can go under.

When there is so much visible change in the world of work it is easy to think of career change as being something forced on people by circumstances beyond their control. However, this is not always the case. There are situations where individuals take matters into their own hands and decide to reshape their working lives themselves.

Proactive change

Proactive change means taking the initiative yourself to start again. The 'trigger' might well be one of the following:

- **ambition** — aiming for a new career which will bring you better rewards (money, power, status etc) in the short or long run;

- **self-development** — broadening the base of your skills to enhance and extend your choice of career in the future; or

- **second thoughts** — realising you are a square peg in a round hole and deciding to do something positive about it.

Reactive change

Reactive change is the more common variety, where change is imposed by external forces, such as:

- **redundancy, downsizing, delayering** — the job you were doing is no longer available, or your skills have become outdated;

- **ill-health** — your employer feels unable to continue your employment because of your poor health record, or, if you have been self-employed, your business has been unable to carry on in your absence; or

● **dismissal** — your employment has been terminated for other reasons. (The manner and reason for your dismissal may affect what sort of job you can consider in the future.)

BEING IN CONTROL

This is all about proactive change, where you are making and taking the decisions yourself.

All of us at some time in our careers become disenchanted with the job we are doing. This is the employment equivalent of the 'seven year itch'. Boredom creeps in. Frustration at lack of promotion opportunities makes us resentful. There's no provision for training. The duties and responsibilities aren't what we expected. We feel undervalued or don't see eye to eye with the boss. The reasons can be many and varied.

Sometimes, it is possible to sort out your dissatisfaction by talking it through with the appropriate head of department and coming to an agreement on what should be done in future. For most people, however, the problem is often overcome by simply walking away from it, and seeking alternative employment with another organisation.

Changing your career as distinct from your employer has nothing to do with the 'seven year itch'. It is a fundamental change. This is why you need to be absolutely clear about what you are doing, and why.

If you are in this situation, ask yourself *precisely* what it is that is making you want to leap into the unknown. Do you genuinely need a new career to reach the top, or just a change of work environment? Is there no way you can extend your skills by taking additional courses in your spare time? How do you know you are a square peg in a round hole? Saying so isn't enough.

Changing direction isn't an easy option: it requires your total commitment; almost always an element of retraining; the possibility of relocation, and a series of potentially crippling financial hurdles to cross. Throwing away a steady job — and your financial security along with it — is fine, as long as you are an independent, single person with no commitments. If you don't fit into this category however, but are still resolutely determined to start again, then you need to be convinced you have *all* of the following:

1. **The wholehearted support of those who are dependent on you**. This does not mean announcing what you intend to do and demanding unquestioning loyalty regardless. Everyone who is directly affected by your decision must be fully aware of what is involved — and

feel able to be supportive. This support could make all the difference between success and failure, so it should never be underestimated.

2. **A financial position solid enough to take the shocks of any unexpected set-backs**. You must be absolutely certain you are not in danger of having your home repossessed if your plans take longer to come to fruition than you anticipated, or that you are likely to reduce your nearest and dearest to a life-style bordering on poverty.

3. **The complete conviction that what you are doing is right, not just for you, but for everyone else who is close to you and affected by your decision**. This means not only being positive in your attitude, but also being realistic. You must be able to back up your assertions with hard, unassailable facts.

TAKING OVER CONTROL

If you have lost your job, for whatever reason, there is a sense of powerlessness — of not being in control. At first, frustration, anger and resentment have to be dealt with. Later, as the initial shock dies down, there can be bitterness or depression. Some people, however, experience a sense of relief once the axe has fallen. Employees in industries and commerce hardest hit by the effects of competitiveness in the global market place, or recurring recessions at home, have often seen the writing on the wall years before the cutbacks or closures begin. For some, the uncertainty of waiting for the inevitable can be harder to cope with than the event itself.

Once the job has gone, controlling what happens in the future passes back to you. The outlook may not be very bright, the opportunities limited, but at least *you* are now in the driving seat. *You* are taking an active part in the decision making process.

Why did I lose my job?
Before deciding what to do next, you need to clarify in your mind exactly why you lost your job, and if there is any way you could avoid this happening again.

Redundancy, downsizing, delayering
Although you might find it hard to appreciate the distinction, in a redundancy situation it is the *job* that is no longer required NOT necessarily the *person* who has been doing it.

Hiring and firing employees is an expensive undertaking. When a job becomes redundant, employers who have invested time and money in attracting good workers don't want to lose them if they can possibly avoid it. They would rather be able to offer alternative work within the organisation, or the chance of retraining if it is appropriate. It is only when these options are not available that the only course open to them is saying 'goodbye'.

There is no guarantee you will be able to protect yourself from being surplus to requirements again at some time in the future. However, there are some questions worth asking yourself in case you unwittingly helped your last employer to decide you should be included in the list of those who had to go. There is no point in making yourself an unnecessarily easy target the next time around.

Answer the questions set out overleaf. If it helps, copy them out and keep them by you as a constant reminder. Remember to answer all the questions honestly. This exercise is for your own use. You are not trying to impress anyone or make excuses.

If you tackle the questions honestly, your answers may provide some clues as to why you and your last employer parted company. It may be that your standard of work or time-keeping affected the decision; perhaps you gave the impression you were inflexible over adopting changes in work practices or taking on board new technology or retraining; or perhaps you were seen as a trouble maker.

You may have good reasons and sound arguments to defend yourself against these accusations, but it is worth pausing for a moment and asking yourself if there was anything at all about your attitude to work, or your superiors, which might have reflected badly on you in the end. If you can spot anything which might hint at this, then bear this in mind when you start your next job, or you could be selecting yourself out of employment once again at some time in the future.

Ill-health

A poor health record can lose you a job. There are limits to how long an employer is prepared to stand the cost of your absence, whether this is the occasional day off every week or so, or a long-term illness lasting several months. It can also apply to situations where your capacity to fulfil all your job requirements has become impaired beyond the point where you can reasonably be accommodated under the employment terms of the Disability Discrimination Act 1995.

If you lose a job through ill-health, make sure it is not your life-style that is contributing to the problem.

Are you smoking or drinking too much? Are you an active sportsman

Can I avoid becoming surplus to requirements again?

1. Was my work/time-keeping always up to the mark?   YES/NO

2. Were there areas I could have improved?   YES/NO

3. If YES, what were they? ....

4. Was I ever told to improve my work/time-keeping?   YES/NO

5. Did I make any effort to do so?   YES/NO

6. If NO, why not?....................................

7. Was there a good working relationship between me and my immediate boss?   YES/NO

8. If NO, why not?....................................

9. Was I ever given the chance to take a training course to help me improve my work skills?   YES/NO

10. If YES, did I take it up?   YES/NO

11. If NO, why not?....................................

12. If there was the chance to take up new ideas/work practices, was I enthusiastic?   YES/NO

13. If NO, why not?....................................

14. Did I ever grumble about the introduction of new work practices?   YES/NO

15. If YES, did I show dissatisfaction?   YES/NO

16. Did I encourage other people to grumble?   YES/NO

17. If YES, was this noticed by my boss?   YES/NO

18. Did I actively show commitment to the organisation?   YES/NO

19. If NO, why not?....................................

20. If I were the boss, would I employ me?   YES/NO

Fig. 1. Checklist: can I avoid becoming surplus to requirements again?

or woman prone to frequent injury on the sportsfield? Is your diet what it should be? Are you taking enough exercise of the right sort? Are you taking drugs? Employers can't be expected to be responsible for your health and safety outside the workplace. That responsibility has to lie with you.

Dismissal

Employment legislation ensures that employers wanting to remove an employee have to follow very precise procedures if they are not to be brought before an employment tribunal for unfair dismissal. Because of this, it should have been made very clear to you at some stage why you are being dismissed or asked to resign.

Dismissal because of your employer's dissatisfaction with some aspect of your work will make it harder for you to obtain a new job, particularly if you are expected to provide references which include your previous employer. So before tackling the job search, you will need to be very certain that whatever the cause of your dismissal, you will not allow yourself to become trapped by the same situation again.

WHY DO I WANT TO CHANGE MY CAREER?

On a clean sheet of paper, write down a single statement why you *need* to make a change. Keep this by you as you work through the various processes in this book. Never forget it.

LOOKING AT THE JOBS MARKET

In the first place, you have to decide whether you need to look for a new career in a totally new environment, or to concentrate on finding broadly similar employment with another organisation. Even if you want to stay in roughly the same type of work, circumstances may prevent you from doing so. There are three points to consider.

1. The restructuring of British manufacturing and service industries since the 1980s.
2. The number of other people in the jobs market who can match your own level of skills and experience.
3. The current level of demand for people with broadly similar skills and experience.

The changing employment market

Was your previous employment in what has now become known as a 'contracting' industry? If it was, then looking for similar employment presents several problems.

- Demand for workers across the whole sector will be declining.
- There will be a large number of job seekers chasing a shrinking pool of jobs.
- Getting another job in the same industry may not protect you from further cutbacks in future.
- Starting with a new employer will leave you vulnerable to the 'last-in-first-out' principle if job cuts are being considered.

Even within the last few years, anyone in this position was being advised to monitor employment trends when planning their next job move.

This way, it was argued, you could avoid or at least reduce the likelihood of future redundancy associated with contracting industries.

Unfortunately, the speed of change can upset the best laid plans. For instance, in this country since the end of World War Two we have seen the decline and collapse of many traditionally labour-intensive industries. Other industries have been lost to competition from abroad. Shipbuilding, coal-mining and steel-making for example, are now employing a tiny fraction of the workforce compared with the vast numbers they used to employ in the past. Here are very obvious examples of contracting industries. But whereas these changes took place over a number of years, and to some extent could be planned for, other shifts in economic activity have taken place over quite short periods of time.

In the late 1980s, the banking and financial sectors of the economy were booming. So were the sunrise industries of the new information technology. These were the 'expanding' job sectors many people were encouraged to target and retrain for. Within two years, however, the onset of a world recession and fluctuations in the UK's economic performance produced a marked reversal of this trend. Cutbacks and redundancies began to appear in job markets insulated against earlier downturns in the economy. Added to this, the rapid technological invasion of nearly every workplace in the last decade has continued to cut swathes through the numbers of employees on companies' payrolls. Looking to the new millennium, the effects of the possible expansion of the EU, the Single Currency, and the impact of the global economy remain unknown quantities. All of them may have profound effects on our career expectations in years to come.

Employment trends therefore are no longer as useful as they once were. They can only give a broad, general guide to future economic activity, *providing nothing unexpected or extraordinary takes place.*

The changing demand for skills

The days when you could find thousands of jobs involving semi-skilled or unskilled work have gone. Automation has replaced human labour and taken away great slices of activity which once involved mundane, routine tasks. Information technology is also beginning to take over in some areas of skilled and professional work, such as quality control and printing, design and administration. Transferable, or portable skills — skills which can be adapted and shaped to meet the requirements of several different types of job — are becoming increasingly important.

If your skills have become outdated in a shrinking market, you must be prepared to retrain if you are to succeed in finding new employment. Progress will not stand still simply to accommodate your need for a job, and there is no Divine Right to employment if you are not prepared to put some effort into it.

You may feel you are too old to learn new tricks. The simple truth is that thousands of people are doing exactly this throughout the country, and the opportunities for retraining or catching up with lost education are expanding all the time. Don't be put off by your age or use this as an excuse: you are never too old to learn — it might just take you a little longer.

Deciding to knuckle down to update or expand your skills is largely a matter of adopting the right attitude, but deciding precisely what skills should be updated or expanded has to be researched very thoroughly, and has a crucial part to play in your campaign to find the right job.

Where does this leave me?

If you know your hopes of getting back into your old type of employment are slim, this is the time to begin putting your future into sharper focus and to start planning with a clearer understanding of what you are trying to achieve. To do this you will need to build on your past.

PLANNING FOR THE FUTURE

Drawing your own Self Portrait

Looking closely at all aspects of your life up to now is a basic and essential part of the career planning process.

Over the next few chapters, you will be considering different aspects of your personal history, starting with your childhood, family and education. Other people should be involved at various stages of this exercise, such as your parents, siblings, colleagues, partners or children — in fact anyone who has played a major part in shaping who, and what, you are.

Other areas to be investigated will include:

- recognising your skills — in the widest sense;
- recognising your strengths and weaknesses, and how to turn both of these to your advantage;
- understanding your true motivational drives, and how these can be used to find a new career;
- recognising the constraints on your freedom of action in choosing a new career — family, finance etc; and
- coming to terms with the options open to you.

To house all the details which will ultimately combine to illustrate your Self Portrait, you will need:

- an A4 ring binder;
- masses of scrap paper;
- pens and pencils;
- an A4 pad;
- a robust folder to house any additional paper etc you may not want to punch holes in, and
- the willingness to spend time and effort on the project.

This last point is crucial. If you don't take the time and trouble to complete each step thoroughly, the end product will not provide you with the essential understanding you need to progress successfully.

At the end of the exercise, you may well discover you have an entirely new perspective on your life — not necessarily a very welcome one. Be prepared for this and for the need to make positive use of all your discoveries, however uncomfortable some of them may be.

As the years go by, a great deal of what we do and achieve fades from our memories: we forget our successes, or the reasons why we chose to do certain things at a particular time. The aim now is to lift these memories out of the attic, dust them off and scrutinise them, because somewhere in the past lie the clues waiting to act as pointers to the future.

CHECKLIST

1. Have you a clear understanding why you are looking for a new career?

2. Do you have the unqualified support of those dependent on you for the action you intend to take?

3. Do you appreciate the reasons why you lost, or lost interest in, your previous line of work?

4. Do these reasons tell you what situations you should avoid in future?

5. Were you employed in a 'contracting' industry?

6. Are your skills sufficiently in demand without needing to be updated?

7. Are the numbers of people seeking employment within your field too great?

8. Could you describe your skills as 'transferable' or 'portable'?

9. Are the openings for these skills only in other industries which are showing signs of contracting?

10. Are there any immediate problems you can identify which at the moment would make retraining difficult?

2

Who Am I?

PUTTING YOURSELF INTO CONTEXT

No matter how much fine detail you put into your Self Portrait, it will be incomplete unless you pay attention to filling in the background. To do this successfully, you need to reflect on several areas of your personal history — your

- family background (parents and siblings)
- educational background and achievements
- personal development outside the education system
- personal preferences in educational subjects
- existing family composition (partner and children).

If you have a partner, encourage him or her to make the same journey into their own childhood. There are three good reasons why you should.

1. By being included in your voyage of discovery, your partner is being brought into the process of change at an early and often vital stage.

2. A partner's involvement can provide support and generate essential discussions which may help you keep a firm grasp on reality.

3. Your partner's previous life experiences might play a crucial role in helping you understand his or her point of view in deciding which future course of action would be best for everyone.

The process of involvement should also be extended to any other resident member of your household. This is particularly important if your career change is likely to involve relocation to another part of the country.

Never forget that what you decide to do about your career could well have a profound effect on everyone around you, whether this person is an elderly relative living with you, or a child reaching a crucial stage in his or her education. You need to know as much about their individual goals and expectations as you do your own. It often takes something as cataclysmic as the enforced or even unenforced career change to highlight the diversity of interests and networks which have been carefully constructed by other members of the family while your attention was focused elsewhere. You ignore these factors at your peril.

YOUR CHILDHOOD FAMILY

Beginnings
The first two questionnaires in this chapter on pages 24 and 25 concentrate on the family you were born into and your place within it. As with all the questionnaires in this book, transfer the headings and the information you list under them onto A4 sheets to be incorporated into your binder as part of your Self Portrait.

Don't skip these questionnaires because you feel the information is irrelevant or unnecessary. Don't skimp on the details either. Your family circumstances when you were a child often have the greatest influence in shaping how you developed as a person, your subsequent outlook on life, and how you now respond to events and other people.

Try to use *all* the questionnaires you are asked to complete not just as fact-finding exercises, although this is important, but also as a basis for reflecting on your life experiences generally.

Reviewing your family history
How much of these questionnaires were you able to complete without asking someone else to corroborate the factual information you needed? Does this tell you anything about your level of awareness of family influences? Is this perhaps an area you should give some thought to?

Sometimes the experience and skills of parents are taken for granted as part of the world we grew up in. Often they get buried beneath the day-to-day demands of family life and remain unrecognised. The simple act of committing the information to paper can help to highlight not just the obvious areas of influence they had on our lives, such as tastes in music, literature or sport, but also the less obvious, such as what life experiences shaped their attitude towards education, work, self-improvement, personal relationships and so on. Delving deeper can be a revelation.

Is there anything in your parents' background which on reflection has affected your own attitude to life? Has this been a positive or negative influence? If this has been a negative input, consider how you might overcome this in future.

The family I grew up in

                                       Father   Mother

Name
Date of birth
Place of birth
Religion
Schools attended

Qualifications gained

Date of marriage
Health
Hobbies/Social activities/
  community/war service

Details of previous marriage
  (if applicable)
Name of partner
Date of marriage
Details of children (names
  and date of birth)

How the marriage ended (death/divorce)
If your parents are no longer married give details . . . .
. . . .
. . . .

Fig. 2. Self-assessment — Who am I?

Me

Full name . . . .

Pet name (if appropriate) . . . .

Date of birth . . . .

Place of birth . . . .

Religion . . . .

Details of brothers and sisters. (Put these in chronological order with date of birth and include yourself to show your position in the family order. Also indicate if any have died and the relevant date.)

1. . . . .

2. . . . .

3. . . . .

4. . . . .

Places where you spent your childhood and which you associate with most.

Describe relationships within the family unit (eg between parents, parents and children, children). Note anything you feel might be relevant.

If there is anything you believe to be important, note it down and keep it with the background questionnaire as part of your Self Portrait. Never discard any random thoughts or ideas. They are often of major importance.

Family traumas
Every family has its ups and downs. Disruption to the comparative calm of everyday life can come in many guises: a death in the family, divorce, remarriage, the arrival of step-children, relocation, the long-term hospitalisation of a parent, brother or sister, parental imprisonment or unemployment. These are just some possibilities that readily spring to mind.

In all probability your childhood will have experienced at least one of the above. Think about what they were. At the time, how aware of these traumas were you? Did any of them take place at a crucial time in your life eg adolescence, or just before you were due to take an important examination? What effect did this have on you then, and why do you think you reacted in the way you did with the benefit of hindsight?

Personal traumas
These are likely to be those events which affected you directly. Consider the following:

● change of schools
● loss of a particular friend
● long-term personal ill-health
● the birth of younger siblings
● the age gap between you and your older/younger siblings
● changes in family relationships as you grew.

Other topics to consider
Here are further ideas to mull over. You will no doubt be able to think of others. Once again, don't disregard anything which now affects the way you look at the world, or your reaction to other people.

● **Were you aware of any family stresses as a child?** Have you since discovered you were shielded from these? If you were, what effect did discovering this have on you at the time of the discovery, and later, on reflection? If you were not shielded, how do you think this affected your own outlook on life?

● **Were there any personal pressures on you to succeed, or to take an adult role before you were ready to do so?** What effect did this have on you?

- **Did the name you were given benefit or hinder you?** Did it colour your behaviour? Would you have preferred to be called something else — and if so, what? What difference do you think it would have made to your life?

- **Have any of your childhood experiences made a lasting impression on you?** What are they and have they been beneficial or detrimental? Which was the most influential?

Summing up

Reflecting on your childhood and your role within the family at the time should provide you with the essentials of who you are and what influences shaped your early years. It should also identify those influences which outlasted childhood and continued to play a part in later years for better or worse. Begin to consider how best you can use these influences now, or whether a shift in attitude might improve your chances of success in the future.

EDUCATION AND LEARNING EXPERIENCES

What have I achieved?

The questionnaire set out on pages 28 and 29 asks you to take a long and comprehensive look at not only your academic achievements, but also the wider learning processes accumulated over the passage of time. These are often either disregarded as irrelevant or underrated and need to be identified and appreciated for what they are — potentially useful life skills.

Don't consciously leave out any skills because you do not see yourself using them in the future. You might never envisage working as a personal assistant again, but shorthand can be a useful tool in many situations, and keyboard skills are increasingly in demand.

Don't overlook the everyday skills that can so often be taken for granted either, such as being able to drive. Leaving out anything can close the door on an option you may never have considered previously. Avoid prejudging the outcome and make sure you have included *everything*, however obscure it might seem.

RECOGNISING YOUR ACHIEVEMENTS

You will almost certainly have a list of accomplishments which is longer than you anticipated when you began the exercise. This can be quite a

My education, training and achievements

Primary and Secondary Education

School	Dates	Achievements (including prizes badges, certificates, qualifications positions held eg team member, member of choir, club membership, prefect etc).

Further Education and Professional Qualifications

Institution and Dates	Course taken	Qualifications and other achievements (including positions held, membership of clubs etc).

Membership of Professional Bodies

Fig. 3. Personal achievements checklist.

Additional educational, training or vocational courses

(Include *any* course you have completed which is not covered by the earlier headings including in-house training, non-academic examinations, those giving you licence to practice, or qualifications. Tick any you did for pleasure rather than out of necessity.)

Date	Course and course content	Exam result or qualification	Studied for pleasure

Of those studied for pleasure, which did you enjoy most and why?

Informal learning

List any skills you have acquired through practice rather than formal training such as those arising from domestic responsibilities, eg counselling; care of the elderly, children, or the handicapped; gardening; decorating; car maintenance, a second language etc.

boost to a deflated ego. As with the earlier questionnaire on your family background, much of what you achieved earlier in your life will have been submerged by later events. In your search for a new career however, nothing must be wasted; everything can have a value. At this stage in the process, it is not always possible to see precisely what this value might be, but it is too early to discount anything. Note it. Keep it.

Areas which might need clarification

Your raw data in itself might not give a clear enough picture. For instance, if you took your examinations over several years then note down next to this information the reason why. Did illness prevent you taking them all at once? Did changing school mean a new syllabus? Did you have to sit some subjects as retakes? Did you get the unexpected opportunity to take an extra subject at a later date?

Think through the reasons why you took the subjects you did in the first place. Was it because:

- you liked them?
- you were good at them?
- your best friend was taking them?
- your parents wanted you to study them? or
- they were essential entry requirements for the university/college course you wanted to follow?

If you went on to further or higher education, also ask yourself the following questions.

- Why did you decide to go on to further/higher education?
- Did you have a career firmly in mind?
- Did you see the course you chose as useful or essential?

Write down your answers to these questions once you are sure of them. The written word can be disarming: there can be no getting away from it, or pushing it out of your mind as you can with an unpalatable thought. Be perfectly honest, something you must be with all these questionnaires if they are to be of any help to you at all.

What your answers might tell you

Some people know from an early age that they want to follow one particular career. They have no qualms or second thoughts and go right ahead and achieve their objective. For most of us, however, the decision is usually less straightforward.

At the time we are asked to make decisions about which subjects to continue and which we should drop, our life experiences are limited. Faced with thousands of possible careers to follow, we have insufficient information or appreciation about what many of these jobs involve. Nor do we have a sound basis for gauging our own future potential. Choices can be made for the flimsiest of reasons with no real understanding of where these might lead us, or more importantly, what career options we might be losing in the process.

Errors of judgement, however valid the reasons seemed to be at the time, can set us off on the wrong path for the rest of our lives — or until we are brought up short by redundancy or a mid-career crisis. If we build on shaky foundations, we shouldn't really be surprised if the construction is wobbly and finally comes tumbling down.

Looking at the reasons why you chose to study particular subjects at school may give you some idea why things did not work out so well later on. Similarly, if you went to college or university uncertain of what you wanted to do with your life at the end of two or three years, there's a good chance that the career you eventually chose was unsuitable.

Don't blame yourself unnecessarily if this is precisely what happened in your own case. Simply recognise that early decisions about what you wanted to do with your working life might have influenced not only your educational choices but also had a considerable part to play in reaching this stage in your career.

Case study: The danger of deciding too soon

At the tender and impressionable age of 8, Simon Capp made a firm decision to become a surgeon. This was entirely due to the experience of witnessing a road accident and his natural instinct of wanting to 'repair' the victim. This set the scene for all Simon's subsequent educational decisions and he worked hard to gain access to medical school and complete his training as a doctor.

Throughout all this time, however, Simon's main obsession was in taking things to bits and repairing them, an obsession reflected in his hobbies. He was an incurable perfectionist and loved to work on the meticulous restoration and renovation of cars, houses and fine instruments. He was never happier than when he was immersed in these solitary, creative tasks.

Simon began to realise that 'repairing' people was not nearly so rewarding to him as repairing things. He recognised he would have been happier in engineering, but lack of mathematical ability prevented him from making the change. Increasingly, he found the stress and pressure of the medical profession too much for him. Combined with a disdain for the pushy style needed to become a consultant, he became increasingly unhappy and reached the point where he positively feared his patients. At 28 years of age, he badly needed a change, wanting most of all a career which reflected his hobbies. Interestingly, as a doctor he was best at practical procedures, such as those involved in chest strains, pleural taps and lumbar punctures.

Simon's motivational drives were all directed towards creative, practical crafts rather than science-based or welfare careers. Whilst he had a high level of intellect which had helped him to succeed in medicine, this was overridden by his interests and personality type. He needed to have an intellectual challenge and to be an expert, but had no urge to compete or climb the ladders of power. He was reserved, traditional and introspective with a need to be self-sufficient. He had little need to forge relationships, impress or connect with people generally. It was little wonder therefore that his time as a doctor had been one which induced in him a state of perpetual tension.

As his hobbies played such an important role in his life, Simon was encouraged to research the possibility of converting these into a full-time career, shifting his medical expertise into a part-time support role.

Simon discovered this was possible. He resigned and enrolled on a three year course in musical instrument making. To support himself, he continued part-time work in dermatology and family planning, but gave this up at the end of his course. By then, he had developed a specialist niche in reproducing medieval harps and 18th century baroque instruments for which there was a growing market. Using the old washroom of his cottage as a workshop he could work in splendid isolation while bringing his work to a wider audience by exhibitions, presentations and lectures.

PERSONAL PREFERENCES IN EDUCATION

Likes and dislikes

How much of what we like or dislike depends on our own personal experience, and how much is a reflection of conditioning by others? Very few of us are immune to other people's opinions, particularly as children. We grow up with examples of gender roles; racial, religious and political attitudes, some of which may take years to overcome or rethink as the personal experience side of our lives comes increasingly into play.

The choice of subjects you studied, or the career you chose may have been affected by parental or social expectations at the time, particularly in relation to what was, or was not, acceptable for a man or woman to do. Even today, in an age of equality of opportunity, gender stereotyping still exists.

Do you think this might have happened in your own case? What else might have influenced you?

To begin with make out five lists, each on a separate sheet of paper:

1. Those subjects you liked studying at school.
2. Those subjects you disliked studying at school.
3. Those subjects you found easy.
4. Those subjects you found difficult.
5. Those subjects you would have liked to study but were unable to.

Think carefully about the categories, or you may make the mistake of putting down subjects in List 1 which really belong to List 3. Just because you found music theory easy, does not necessarily mean you enjoyed doing it. Similarly, don't confuse disliking a subject with problems you had in mastering it.

Leave aside List 5 for the moment. Go through each of the first four lists in turn and ask yourself *why* the subject appears on the list it does. Here are some possible reasons:

- The lessons were good fun/boring.
- The teacher always picked on me.
- I always did well/badly at exams.
- I was good/bad at practical work.
- Everyone had to do it.

It may become clear to you that the reason you liked or disliked a particular subject had nothing to do with your ability or even your level of interest. Perhaps it had everything to do with the way the subject was taught or the relationship that existed between you and your teacher. Go through your list again if you can find instances of this and ask yourself if you might have felt differently about the subject if it had been taught by a different teacher at the time. Do you think this might have affected your choice of subjects studied in later years?

Lastly, return to List 5 and write down the reasons why you were unable to study this subject, and more importantly, why you wanted to study it in the first place. Later on in the discovery process, when considering which career path to follow in future, this may be a vital piece in the picture.

YOUR FAMILY NOW

The last piece of work on your Self Portrait at this stage is to look at the composition of your present family, and the existing networks of those closest to you. Some of the information asked for in the questionnaire on pages 35 and 36 will have been provided already if your partner and other dependants have completed the earlier questionnaires with you, but there are residual questions which still need to be answered. Involvement of everyone who is capable of being involved is crucial to avoid inadvertently overlooking any aspect of someone's life which he or she regards as vitally important.

Considering the needs of your present family

A review of your family's connections and commitments at an early stage has the obvious advantage of giving you adequate warning of likely problem areas in future. The most obvious dangers are damaging a partner's career, or the examination chances of your children if you have to seriously consider not just moving house, but relocating to another part of the country. It is quite pointless actively considering a post in the Outer Hebrides if you know the rest of your family has its roots going down to the bedrock of the Isle of Wight.

It may be that financial pressures might force you to seriously consider such a drastic move, but before you do, you will have to be sure there are no other options open to you. There is no mileage in pretending consultation doesn't matter. A family uprooted and dumped in what they regard as a 'hostile' environment may take months or even years to settle, if ever. The ultimate price of your autocratic decision may turn out to be an educational disaster for your children, a partner contemplating separation, or an elderly relative constantly pining for the loss of familiar faces and places. So take note of what you are told and appreciate there are others in the family unit with their own fears and uncertainties besides yourself.

CHECKLIST

1. Have you completed all the questionnaires in this chapter honestly and to the best of your ability?

2. Have you involved all those who should be consulted?

3. Were there any details about your childhood that you had not been aware of up to this time?

My family unit today

Partner

Name   . . . .

Date of birth   . . . .

Place of birth   . . . .

Religion   . . . .

Education

Secondary School College/University	Dates	Educational Achievements

Professional qualifications

Recent Career History

Job Title	Dates	Duties and Responsibilities

Hobbies, membership of clubs and leisure interests

Additional skills

Fig. 4. Family questionnaire.

Children (tick those still living at home)

Name	Date of birth	School, college, university or place of work

Hobbies, membership of clubs and leisure interests

Additional information (such as dates of important examinations, health problems) . . . .

Other relatives living in your household
Name(s)

Relationship

Date(s) of birth

Religion(s)

Occupation(s) (if relevant)

Hobbies, membership of clubs, leisure interests

List all those who would have to move with you if you relocated within the next twelve months.

Fig. 4. continued.

4. If so, do these make any material difference to your outlook on life?

5. Have you discovered anything about your decisions to study particular subjects either at school or at college which you feel might be relevant to your current difficulties?

6. If so, do you feel these are important enough to be taken into consideration when looking for a new career?

7. Have you discovered anything about your partner's accomplishments/commitments you were unaware of until this exercise?

8. If so, do you appreciate what the significance of these might be in relation to your efforts to start a new career?

9. Have you discovered anything about your children's lives or those of any other dependent relative living with you that will also affect the way you approach your career search?

10. If so, are you prepared to accommodate their expectations within the planning stage of your career search?

3

Drawing on Work Experience

The next part of your Self Portrait is looking in depth at your work experience. This means not just *what* jobs you did, but *why* you did them; what you liked or disliked about them; what you think you might like to do in the future; and finally, what might prevent you from making your dreams become a reality.

WHAT JOBS HAVE I DONE?

The questionnaire on page 39 should be completed now. This will be the working document you will be using as a reference point for the remainder of the chapter.

You will see that you are asked to work forward in time rather than the reverse. There is a sound reason for this. The questionnaire is not meant to be an application form or a curriculum vitae. Both of these nowadays place greater emphasis on the last position held and give less prominence to earlier employment. The questionnaire however, is meant to do the opposite; to take you through your career history from its earliest, perhaps humble beginnings, and by doing so to help you examine your reasons for moving on to the next job. Make the record as comprehensive as possible. Include your very first paper round if necessary, and any periods of work experience for which you did not get paid.

ANALYSING YOUR WORK HISTORY

Type of jobs

Your list may give you a very clear picture of the type of job you have always gone for, such as clerical, selling, marketing, physically demanding, computing etc. If there is no consistency in your pattern of *type*, is there any consistency of work environment which could be seen as a pattern? For instance, were you desk-bound or mobile, indoors or outdoors? Were you working in isolation or as part of a team? Were you one of many, or one of a few?

Patterns are important when considering what action to take in future.

My working history and experience

(Start with your very first job and work forwards in time. Also include any periods of employment or work experience for which you did not get paid, and any part-time or temporary employment.)

Dates	Job title and name of employer	Duties and responsibilities	Reason for leaving

---

Fig. 5. Working history and experience.

You may have had a marked preference for a particular working environment. Conversely, you may have had a marked loathing for it too. Which was it? Think about this carefully. Make notes of anything which you feel is relevant or important.

Duties and responsibilities

What happened to the level of duties and responsibilities you undertook over the years? Did they increase rapidly during your early years of employment and then flatten out as time went by, or was there a steady increase over the whole period? Whichever is true, were you happy with this state of affairs, or would you have liked to see a different pattern if you had had the choice?

Looking ahead, consider what level you would ultimately like to work at in your new career. Do you want more responsibility, less or roughly the same? Make a note of what you decide.

Looking at your first job in detail

For this part of the exercise it is important to consider your first full-time, fully paid employment.

Why did you choose this particular job? Write down your answer and consider the implications. State precisely *why* you wanted the job in preference to any other. Here are some possibilities:

- It sounded interesting.
- The money was good.
- My best friend was working with the same company.
- They were recruiting art graduates.
- The training programme was good.
- If you worked hard you could get promotion quickly.
- It was the only job going at the time.
- I couldn't think of anything else.
- My father/mother/parents wanted me to take it.

Like picking subjects to study at school, any of the above reasons may have been perfectly valid at the time, but with hindsight some of them are hardly the stuff on which to build solid foundations for a future career. Ask yourself what effect this first choice had on the rest of your career. Was it a mistake? Did you recognise it and change course or did you just plough on regardless and make the best of a bad job? If you had your time over again, would you make the same choice — and why? Once again, write down your thoughts so that nothing is overlooked later.

Case study: Educating yourself into a cul-de-sac

Susan French (31) obtained a degree specialising in Scandinavian languages and went on to gain additional secretarial qualifications and Teaching English as a Foreign Language. After qualifying, she automatically chose office work as a natural consequence of her studies and obtained numerous secretarial jobs through an agency.

However, she was never completely at ease in her secretarial role. What she enjoyed most was helping out at a children's home in her spare time, particularly with the craft work and she began to question whether or not she had chosen the right direction for her career.

Her dissatisfaction with her choice of work increased until she decided to seek professional careers advice to give her some much needed guidance.

Her assessment results showed that she was highly motivated towards welfare or caring careers but with the additional need for academic work.

These findings reinforced what Susan herself already knew at heart, that she would only be happy working with people and that she had the academic ability to tackle whatever job she set her mind to.

With this in mind, she took a job as a 'helper' in an Occupational Therapy Department with the intention of moving up the promotional ladder to a higher grade.

The pros and cons of each job

Every job has its good and bad points. The next part of the exercise is to work your way through all the jobs on your questionnaire, including the casual, temporary or part-time ones you have listed.

Take yourself back to the time you were doing that particular job. Remember the work environment, the people you worked with and those you worked under. Remind yourself of what was involved in the day-to-day duties and responsibilities of the job itself. Take this further and reflect on the whole period you were employed on this job. Did it work out the way you expected when you started? Did anything happen which affected your attitude towards the job later on? Was this good or bad? Did it ultimately make you decide you wanted to look elsewhere for new employment?

Having refreshed your memory about the job, now make two lists under the headings 'Likes' and 'Dislikes'. The following list is a rough guide to areas of the job which could be usefully analysed. You can add others which might be relevant in your own case.

● **Aspects of the job content**. Identify specific duties you liked or disliked.

- **Level of responsibility**. State why you liked or disliked the level of responsibility attached to the post.

- **Work environment**. Restrict your comments to the place rather than the people.

- **Colleagues**. Divide this group into three: subordinates, peer group and bosses. Put names to the people you list and say why you liked or disliked them.

- **Pay structure**. State what was good or bad about it.

- **Hours of work.** State your reasons for liking or disliking the system you had to work.

- **Holidays**. Was there anything about the conditions under which you had to take your holidays which were good or bad as far as you were concerned?

Finally, write down what you liked *most* about the job, and what you liked *least*.

Complete this exercise for every job individually *using the same headings* and compare your notes.

What do these lists tell me?
Both lists have their uses, so don't just concentrate on the 'Likes' and forget about the 'Dislikes'.

The list of 'Likes' should give you a rough idea what gives you the most satisfaction from any job. Identifying the one aspect of the job you liked most is also a pointer to what you should be looking for in future. *But this is only a pointer*. What you liked most might be nothing more than the best of an indifferent set of circumstances rather than an essential requirement of any future career.

The list of 'Dislikes' should be used as a warning to remind you of aspects of past jobs you found irksome, or worse. Take note of these and weigh up their importance, or their significance. Pay attention to the aspect you liked least because once again this is a pointer. It tells you clearly what you should avoid in future if possible.

Where your greatest 'Like' or 'Dislike' involved colleagues, this means you are more likely to place greater store on working relationships than the content of the work itself, or the environment in which it takes place. Interpersonal chemistry is a mysterious human process and is something which unfortunately is often impossible to evaluate until you start a job. The only exception to this is when you are interviewed by your potential boss and you know immediately there is something about him or her which would set your teeth on edge if you had to work with them.

Which job did I enjoy most?

Looking through your job list, select one job taken all round you enjoyed the most. Include in your consideration the complete job list on your questionnaire and not just the full-time paid positions you have held.

Don't be put off selecting one of the casual or temporary posts: in this exercise, every post has to be given equal consideration as the next. If you find yourself choosing one of these 'lesser' posts, you have signalled there was something about the job which was important and needs to be recognised when planning your future career. Equally, in making your choice, don't automatically pick your last job. It may represent the pinnacle of your career so far, but it may not represent the one which gave you the most personal satisfaction.

When you have decided, write down your choice and say why, when you look back over your career history, this job means more to you than all the rest. Think over the implications of what you have written. Are there any surprises? Have you finally revealed something to yourself you have been hiding away for years?

LOOKING AHEAD

What would I like to do in the future?

Having concentrated on the past, it is now time to let your imagination run riot and think about the future. This part of the exercise is all about what you *want* to do, not what you *can* do.

Commit your thoughts to paper. Be honest with yourself and don't rule out anything on the grounds that it sounds silly, or too outlandish. At this stage, anything goes, from flights of pure fantasy to cherished notions you have held for years but have never dared admit to. Remember, if your Self Portrait is to reflect a true likeness of yourself, you can't afford to cheat on details.

What happens if you can't identify a particular career immediately? Don't worry. In fact, trying to pin yourself down to any particular career at this stage might well be too restricting. Adopt the broad brush approach if this helps, using all-embracing ideas such as –

I want to look after animals.
I don't want to be stuck in an office.
I want to travel.
I'd like to help people.
I want to control my own working day.
I want to be creative.

Put down as many ideas as possible, expanding on the one before if you can to begin the process of fine-tuning the original thought. Start to put your ideas into a working environment.

For instance, take the first example — 'I want to look after animals.' Think about in what context.

- Do you want to care for them when they are sick?
- Have you any particular type of animals in mind?
- Do you want to rear them?
- Do you want to look after them on a nine-to-five basis or at any time?
- Do you want to be part of a conservation or animal welfare group?
- Would you want to work indoors, outdoors or a bit of both?

From these answers, a whole range of potential career openings begin to emerge.

- Veterinary surgeon or nurse.
- Groom, stable or kennel hand.
- Zoo keeper.
- Farmer, stockman or shepherd.
- Fish farmer.
- Ranger or conservationist.
- Butcher.
- RSPCA Inspector.
- Animal charity worker.

As you can see, the range of possibilities is surprisingly large. It can range from the humble to the exalted, the practical to the theoretical, the office-based to the outdoor, the national to the international.

Let yourself go. Brainstorm if necessary, and see what you have got hidden away in the inner recesses of your mind that you haven't dared admit to yourself until now. Write it all down on paper: it can't escape your grasp if you do. It's there, a tantalising glimpse of a possible future.

At the end of the exercise you may still not be able to pin down precisely what you want to do. You may only have a very rough idea what you want from the world of work. Don't worry, the next chapter will help to fill in more of the detail you need to complete your picture.

If you have a very firm idea of what career you want to follow however — it may have been your deepest wish ever since you left school but circumstances prevented you from following it up — admit to it. Say it. Write it down. 'I want to be a . . . '.

Now, what's stopping you?

What is stopping me?

This is where reality creeps in. This is the point where your feet have to be firmly rooted to the ground. It does not necessarily mean your goal becomes unattainable, it may just have to be achieved over a longer period of time or by a more circuitous route, but it has to be recognised there are situations which make it impossible or difficult for you to achieve your aim.

Unrealistic targets

There are quite obviously some careers which are forever closed to us if we lack the basic essential talent for them, have physical limitations or are hampered by the times we live in.

No amount of wanting to become a famous violinist will be of any use if, despite endless practice and tuition, you fail to master the instrument. Nor is there any point in hankering after becoming a fire fighter if you have defective vision or a physique which does not come up to the required standards. Equally as futile is the longing to be involved in the terraforming of Mars: you can do nothing except resign yourself to the simple fact that you have been born too soon.

Wrong qualifications

This is a problem which usually dates back to decisions we made in our mid-teens about which subjects we were good at and should keep studying, and which subjects we were bad at and should drop.

This simplistic approach can be very persuasive. Subjects get dropped which might prove vital to your career prospects in later life. You would have been better advised to keep as broad a mix of subjects as the curriculum would allow and offered extra tuition in those you found difficult.

If you are faced with a situation where your qualifications, or lack of them, is likely to bar your progress, there is no need to despair. Every year, thousands of people start from scratch to make up the deficiencies of their earlier education. There is a stunning array of the provision available for the mature student, with or without relevant qualifications. Only in circumstances where the time taken to qualify is long-term, and the number of years available to you to practise your new career before retirement is limited, are there any upper age barriers to block your way.

Other sources of information include your local Careers Office, college or Training and Enterprise Council (or Local Enterprise Company in Scotland).

Writing to the professional body of the career which interests you will also produce information, not only on what entry qualifications will be required, but any additional study which might be expected if you are to gain full professional status.

Inadequate skills or experience

This too is not necessarily an insurmountable problem. If you are considering going back to study, periods of work experience in sandwich courses or additional work taken on during the vacation periods may well be sufficient to give you an acceptable grounding.

Personal approaches to businesses or organisations in the field you are interested in may also provide you with suggestions on how to gain additional skills or experience.

The Training and Enterprise Councils (TECs) in England and Wales, or the Local Enterprise Companies (LECs) in Scotland run a variety of courses to improve skills training for the unemployed. These include short duration taster courses to give you the chance to decide whether the field you have chosen is the right one for you.

Getting involved with voluntary work in the area which interests you is also a good way of making up lost ground, particularly in caring roles.

Too old

Despite the lack of any law against age discrimination and the tendency by many employers to look for younger people, it is by no means a universal trend. Many employers are coming to realise older, more mature employees appeal to the growing number of older, more mature customers.

In most cases, age has nothing to do with making a fresh start. It can of course limit the amount of time you have available to reach the top, but if reaching the top is not your aim, then don't persuade yourself this is an adequate reason. As the Open University roll of students amply demonstrates, you are never too old to learn — it might just take you a little longer.

Lack of confidence

If you have been employed by a single organisation all your working life, or in the same type of work, starting out into the unknown can be a daunting prospect. The experience of losing your job and the self-doubt that accompanies this can strangle your sense of adventure, consciously or unconsciously. There is a terrible tendency to talk yourself down, or to concentrate on the negative side of life. This not only puts off prospective employers and friends, it has a debilitating effect on your own mental well-being.

There is no easy answer to this problem except trying to adopt a more positive approach to your new job search, secure in the knowledge that you are doing the right thing both for yourself and your family. Being sure is the hard part, which is why you are about the business of unravelling your past to build a more solid future.

Family or other commitments

These are genuine difficulties which have to be considered in detail. For instance, it is no good glossing over the problems of being a full-time or even a part-time student if you have young children: you may miss out on crucial periods of their development; you may be placing too great a burden on your partner in confining the caring role to one person, or jeopardise his or her career in the process. In other words, you may be storing up stresses and strains which will ultimately lead to family breakdown or divorce.

Other commitments can be equally demanding: the weekly meeting of the youth club you organise; the number of days you are obliged to sit as a magistrate; the local branch committee meetings of your professional body; or your stint recording the local paper onto tapes for the blind. Whatever your commitments, evaluate each one carefully and aim to retain your links with only those you believe are vital. For those which have to take a back seat for a while, explain the reasons for your temporary unavailability and keep in touch. Don't be tempted to drop them completely. Any network of contacts and connections you have built up in the past might prove valuable in the future.

Finance

Combined with the difficulties you are likely to encounter with family and other commitments, financing yourself and your dependants through a period of change can sometimes be the main obstacle to retraining or starting afresh. Surviving on a mature student's grant or having to finance your own period of study can be a harrowing experience.

Because this is a topic which needs looking at in detail, the whole of Chapter 9 is devoted to it.

Attitude

Don't let your approach to a new career be dogged by a negative attitude or excuses which boil down to simply not wanting to put yourself out to make the effort. If you aren't prepared to put anything into your search for a new beginning, then you can't expect to get anything worthwhile out of it at the end.

CHECKLIST

1. Have you taken care to include *all* your work experience in the questionnaire?

2. Have you identified a pattern in the type of work you have done previously?

3. Have you been able to clarify your reasons for taking your first full-time permanent job? If so, with hindsight are you satisfied it was the right choice?

4. What have you discovered about your 'likes' and 'dislikes' in the various jobs you have had over the years?

5. Does this knowledge give you any clear pointers which you should take into account when considering a new career?

6. Which were the factors you considered to be most important when you picked out the job you enjoyed most?

7. What ideas for possible future careers have you generated from your brainstorming session?

8. What obstacles have you identified which might prevent you following any of these as a career?

9. What measures can you take, if any, to overcome these problems?

10. Are the obstacles genuine, or simply excuses for inaction?

4

Building on Hobbies and Interests

MOTIVATIONAL DRIVES

Why these are so important

What you do in your spare time is a far better indicator of the type of working environment you prefer than your career history. Why is this?

The answer is simple — you take up a hobby or an interest because you *want* to, not because you *have* to. Perhaps when you were younger, and your parents did your thinking for you, they decided it would be a good idea if you joined the Brownies/Cubs, or went to ballet classes or football training. Once you were old enough to have your own say in the matter however, your personal choices took over from parental ones. They may have been similar; they may have been completely different; but the big difference was they were *your own*.

The motivation behind your decision to spend time doing one thing rather than another is unique to you: you are motivated to do something because you enjoy what you are doing, and you enjoy doing it because it fits in very precisely with your own preferences. If it didn't, you would stop doing it and take up something else.

Looking for the right career means identifying these motivational drives, understanding their significance and transferring them to the workplace.

Case study: Trying to be someone you're not

Amy Howard was 26. Her main hobby was gardening. She loved it. Despite having lots of other hobbies, gardening and garden design had played a very large part in her life but she had never felt confident enough to pursue the idea that she could make a career out of it.

Amy was the child of academic parents. She went to university and gained a BA in English. Subsequently she had a succession of jobs primarily as a hostel worker for homeless young people. Wanting a change to something more creative she resigned and joined a theatre company, also attending evening classes in art, pottery, screen printing and writing.

As time passed, the need for financial security became increasingly important to her and her initial reaction was to turn again to community work. Her attempts to get back into this type of employment however, met with no success and she began to wonder if she might not be better trying her hand at something completely different.

Amy's motivational drives confirmed her main interests lay in practical rather than caring careers. She had been a successful social worker only because she was capable of being calm in a crisis. However, she had fared less well when needing to be assertive.

It was clear Amy had a strong liking for working with tools and materials and producing tangible results. She also had a need for artistic expression. Combined with indications that she would be able to cope with self-employment, everything pointed towards her making the most of one of her hobbies, in this case either pottery or gardening.

Amy was encouraged to consider several options including courses in agriculture and horticulture. Two years later she had started up her own gardening and garden design and construction business, and was also involved in teaching the subject at adult education classes.

EARLY INTERESTS

Influence during your school years

Although some of your earlier interests might have been parent or teacher inspired, not all of them will necessarily have been discarded in later life. Interests kindled during childhood can expand and develop with the passing years into related hobbies, or become springboards into others. For this reason it is important to take them into account to appreciate the development which might have taken place, and what signposts they may offer from an employment point of view.

When you complete Part I of the questionnaire on page 51 put in as much detail as possible. Include membership of clubs or societies and any status or merit achieved, such as captain of a team, school team member, badges obtained, trophies won, first violin etc. Here you have the basis for the interests you developed in later years.

Before moving on to Part II, identify the hobbies or interests you enjoyed most. Did you have a particular favourite? What was it? Are you still involved with this interest in some way? Are there any you regret giving up? Would you like to take them up again if the opportunity presented itself? As always, write down the answers for future reference.

LATER INTERESTS

Membership of clubs and associations since leaving school

List your later affiliations in date order in Part II of the questionnaire. Highlight any official roles you held, and for how long. Also include in

Hobbies and interests

Part I — Childhood
Age 4 – 11 years

Subject/Club Society	What was involved and achievements	Age when discontinued	Reason for discontinuing

Age 12 – 18 years

Subject/Club Society	What was involved and achievements	Age when discontinued	Reasons for discontinuing

Part II — Membership of clubs and associations since leaving school

Dates	Name of club/society/ association	Official roles	Reason for discontinuing

Fig. 6. Hobbies and interests list.

this section any formal or informal groups you joined with your colleagues, on or off work premises which were social in nature, such as a darts or quiz team, a rambling group or social club.

As you did with Part I, look through the later list of activities. Once again, was there any interest which was a clear favourite, and why? Do you regret having given anything up? Is there anything preventing you from taking it up again now or in the future?

PERSONAL INITIATIVES

Self-motivation is a powerful force. Harnessed to a particular goal or project, it can achieve wonders. It is particularly useful in a situation where you are aiming to achieve something new and where your success is likely to depend on your personal level of drive and determination.

Bearing this in mind, is there anything in your past which you took it upon yourself to organise or initiate? It doesn't matter how young you were at the time, or how trivial it might seem now on reflection. It might have been something as simple as raising money for a charity collection at school, or putting on a puppet play to entertain your friends. Add it to your list. The fact that you initiated it is what counts.

In compiling your list of personal initiatives, work forward from your school days up to the present time. Include anything which might be connected with the social side of your employment, such as departmental quiz teams, firms' dances or staff magazines. Don't however, include anything which directly relates to work practices themselves. The motivation for initiating action in the workplace is often triggered by other influences, such as a company's expectations of its employees or a generous bonus payments system. If you had had exactly the same job with a different employer, you might never have had the necessary stimulus to generate the idea, so include only those activities which were self-motivated.

As you make your list, write down what part you played and whether it changed. Did your role remain solitary, or did you delegate and become part of a team? Is there a pattern in how you handle your initiatives? Both the initiative and your way of building on it are good indicators of how you like to work.

YOUR MAIN INTERESTS NOW

What you enjoy doing most in your spare time
Moving on to your present interests, stick to those which you can honestly say are of real interest to you. Don't include activities which have

been allowed to slip over the years, or those you participate in so infrequently they really cannot be said to play a major part in your life. Use as a guideline a regular commitment of your time on a daily, weekly or monthly basis.

The next questionnaire on your interests on page 55 has been divided into three parts:

- hobbies
- leisure pursuits
- voluntary work/commitments.

For the purposes of this exercise, it is useful to make a clear distinction between these three headings. Understand what these distinctions are before you complete the questionnaire.

Why the distinction?

Hobbies and leisure pursuits are terms which are often confused. They are however quite distinct and for the purpose of this exercise this distinction should be recognised for the following reasons:

1. To identify your additional skills or specialised knowledge which could be built on to provide a new career.

2. To separate the very different motivational drives behind your choice of spare time activities which need to be taken into account.

Hobbies

Hobbies are activities: they are pastimes in which the stimulus is from within yourself. You play squash or swim. You are a do-it-yourself addict or cook. You collect stamps or raise gardenias. You write fiction or paint watercolours. You are motivated to do something.

Hobbies usually require a *skill* of some sort or *specialised knowledge*. This skill or knowledge may only be minimal, or it may be on a par with that of an expert; it may have been acquired by watching others, by personal trial and error, by practice or by taking lessons — but you have been motivated to acquire it, which is why it is special.

Leisure pursuits

Leisure pursuits are precisely that: the pursuit of leisure. They are pastimes in which you have no active part to play: someone else is providing the stimulus. You watch television or listen to music. You go to the theatre or the cinema. You are a football supporter or avid reader of fiction.

Your motivation in these situations is quite different. You are seeking the opportunity to sink yourself into another world for a while — to take a break. You are a spectator. It is not essential to have a basic skill or specialised knowledge. You can enjoy the experience for its own sake.

Voluntary work or commitments
Your level of motivation to do unpaid work within the community is another useful guide to your personality and preferences. Like your hobbies, it demands activity on your part, but this time the direct benefit is felt by others and not yourself. You may have the indirect benefit of getting personal satisfaction from doing the work, but this is only because it has given pleasure, or helped to make somebody's life a little easier. There has to be feedback from someone else.

Community work might involve a local branch of a national charity, or a group which has sprung up from within the community itself to meet a particular need. Or it may be a personal commitment you have taken on board which is not the responsibility of any organised group, such as regular shopping for an elderly neighbour, providing transport to and from hospital etc.

Completing the questionnaire
When listing the skills or specialist knowledge involved in a particular hobby, or in community roles, make this as comprehensive as possible, including physical skills. For example –

tennis:

- fast reflexes
- good eye/hand co-ordination
- controlled arm movement
- an understanding of the rules of the game
- strategy
- stamina
- an appreciation of team work (doubles)

secretary of a local charity:

- good administration (minute taking, letter writing, committee organisation, working to deadlines, methodical)
- office skills (shorthand/typing, word processing, use of duplicator/photocopier/telephone, keeping filing system)

My spare time interests today

Hobbies

Hobby	Duration of interest	Time spent per week etc	Skills or specialist knowledge needed

Leisure pursuits

Leisure pursuit	Duration of interest	Time spent per week etc	Reason for interest

Voluntary work or commitment

Type of work and name of organisation	Duration of interest	Time spent per week etc	Skills or specialised knowledge needed

Fig. 7. Current spare time interests.

- social skills (good listener, good communicator, diplomatic)
- able to work unsupervised
- able to work as part of a team.

As you can see from the above examples, you probably possess many more skills and far more knowledge than you ever gave yourself credit for.

PERSONAL PREFERENCES IN A SOCIAL CONTEXT

When you have completed your questionnaire, study the individual hobbies, leisure pursuits and the work you do in the community.

Ask yourself the following questions for each hobby etc and write down the answers.

1. Is the activity something you do on your own or in a group?
2. If it is a group activity, does it involve a single sex or a mixed sex group?
3. If it is a group activity, does it involve large numbers of people you might not know, or a small close-knit group of friends?
4. Is the activity indoor or outdoor?
5. Do you have to relate quickly to people you do not know?

Is there a regular pattern of preference or not? Do you always mix socially with a large number of other people? Are you happier on your own? Do you naturally gravitate towards certain groups? Are you the indoor or outdoor type? These are the sort of questions you can ask yourself.

From your answers, do you think your preferences can be transferred into a working environment? Conversely, are there some obvious work situations you would now want to avoid?

Making a choice

If you had to choose only *one* of your current spare time interests, which would it be? Think about this very carefully before you choose. Write down your decision and then state as fully as possible why you have made this choice.

Look at what your choice means in terms of the skills and abilities needed; the social context in which it takes place; and the personal motivation behind why you enjoy your involvement.

If you have chosen honestly, the item selected should provide you with one of the best indicators yet of the type of work you should be considering and the most appropriate working environment to suit you.

Reasons for doing what you do

Having looked at the social side of your spare time interests, turn next to *why* you do them.

Look through the questionnaire again. Select from the list below, the best description of the *motive* that lies behind your involvement. If you do something because you enjoy being a leader or because you are ambitious to achieve, don't be ashamed to admit it. This is your Self Portrait. It must reflect who you are. Write down the letters identifying your motives next to each interest and add up how many of each set of letters you have at the end. You may find you need to use more than one set to describe your reasons fully.

- self-expression   (SE)
- social contact   (SC)
- helping others   (HO)
- authority over others   (AO)
- personal challenge   (PC)
- prestige value   (PV)
- individual freedom   (IF)

Is there any one motive which is the clear leader, or is there a mix? Does this give you any clues about the sort of job and working environment you would feel comfortable in?

PERSONAL PREFERENCES IN THE CONTEXT OF YOUR JOB

Your motivational drives can be expressed in other terms — as qualities you display as part of your approach to your job. For example:

- Self-expression   = creative
- Social contact   = team orientated
- Helping others   = caring
- Authority over others   = able to lead
- Personal challenge   = achievement orientated
- Prestige value   = seeking a high profile
- Individual freedom   = self-sufficient

Very often you see these qualities being asked for in job advertisements. For example — 'We are looking for someone who is able to work under pressure to a high standard as part of our dynamic sales force.' Roughly translated this means — 'We are looking for an achiever who can work as part of a team.'

Translate your own motivational drives into qualities which might be sought by an employer and write out a brief paragraph incorporating these in an advertisement for a fictitious vacant post.

CHECKLIST

1. What hobbies and interests from your childhood have shaped your adult interests?

2. Were these childhood interests self-generated, or through parental or other adult influences?

3. Has personal initiative played a dominant role in your spare time pursuits?

4. Have you learnt more about your range of skills and abilities by scrutinising your various interests?

5. If so, have you identified any which you feel might become transferable skills in the job market?

6. Does the total amount of time you spend on your hobbies etc each week almost match the amount of time you used to spend at work?

7. Do you regard these outside activities as being less important/just as important/more important than work?

8. Do you feel you have learnt anything about the sort of environment, level of activity and social mix that appeals to you most?

9. If so, do you feel you could translate this into what you would like to see in a new career?

10. Are you also clearer in your mind what work situations you now need to avoid?

5

How Do Others See Me?

STEPPING OUTSIDE YOURSELF

This chapter puts the finishing touches to your Self Portrait. Up to now you have been delving into your history, extracting your many and varied experiences, identifying your skills and abilities, and considering the motivational drives that make up who you are. You have been studying your special uniqueness.

Looked at as a whole, this exercise may have thrown up one or two surprising results: you may have cast a completely different light on events in your past, or your capabilities in the present; you may now feel some regret over certain actions, or satisfaction over the outcome of others. You may also have begun to feel more positive about making better use of the future.

The aim of this chapter is to stand back and study your finished picture. You should now feel confident you know yourself much better than you did before you began the exercise. But what about other people? They only see the finished 'portrait', not what went into its making. This can colour their attitude towards you and their perception of you as a person.

So what do they see? Does everyone 'see' the same person? Do you think you might make more of what you have to offer if you changed the 'image' in some way?

To answer these questions, you need to stand away from yourself and analyse how other people react to you in different situations, how this can affect your approach to them, and what you can learn from this interaction.

LIFE ROLES AND ROLE PLAY

It is true to say all of us show different images of ourselves to the outside world depending on the circumstances we face at the time. You can think of these various personae as a series of masks, if you like. The 'real' us lying behind these masks may never be revealed to others, or may only be revealed at a time of crisis. This can present us with a problem: if we aren't careful, we can begin to live the life of the person *other people imagine we are*, because this is what they expect of us. This expectation can place a tremendous strain on the individual concerned, especially if he or she is effectively having to live a lie to match these expectations.

We all play a large number of roles in the course of our everyday life — rather like quick-change parts in a play — but we can only be successful in these roles if we feel comfortable in them. Playing a part we do not feel 'at home' in, lowers our stress threshold and can make life unbearable after a while.

Roles within the family

Start at the beginning and think about the most obvious roles you have to play in life — those connected with your childhood place within a family, and the transition from childhood to adulthood with its changing demands. These are:

- child
- lover
- partner
- parent.

The child's role

In its simplified form, this is a role where you are subservient, totally dependent on others and need to be cared for and loved.

Your views are rarely if ever taken into consideration. You are expected to listen to older or more experienced people and be guided by them. You are not expected to take the initiative. You are instructed on what action to take and expected to carry this out. If you act your part well, you receive love and affection. If you do not, you run the risk of having these much-needed responses taken away. You are very vulnerable.

Some people carry this role into the adult world, usually with disastrous results.

The lover's role

The lover's role has a large element of the child in it: you are dependent and need to be loved. The difference here is that your part is not played for general consumption: it is aimed at one person — the object of your desire who has some power over you. But the subservience you display is no longer childlike: it is no longer total. There is the expectation that at some stage the other party will reciprocate, so that the power to hold in thrall will pass back and forth, like a weight being passed between the two sides of a pair of scales.

It is when this mutual passing back and forth stops that you are left with an imbalance: one person has the ascendancy over the other. The role and the mask that goes with it has changed: you have become either the 'parent' or the 'child' on a permanent basis and the relationship becomes unstable and usually comes to an end.

The partner's role

The partner's role in generalised terms is one of mutual support. You play a variety of parts to suit a variety of circumstances. You can expect to play the lover, the child or the parent, depending on the situation. Equally, you will expect your partner to play the reciprocal role to maintain the balance of the partnership. Equilibrium is maintained when both parties understand their roles, and respond to situations by adopting the right reciprocal role for the occasion. Disequilibrium sets in as soon as one partner does not accept the role he or she is required to play by the other and the element of partnership collapses.

The parental role

This role is a mixture of care, protection and dominance. You are the initiator of actions, the leader, the decision-maker, the controller of others. Subordination is all around you. You expect to be listened to and your advice to be acted upon. You may achieve your ends with a velvet glove or a mailed fist, but this is no way affects the outcome. You may be extremely caring and thoughtful of others, but you are nevertheless the one who is very much in charge.

Some people take the autocratic side of the parental role out of the family and into the wider world. This is the role that in the wrong hands and unmodified by other behavioral roles inevitably causes conflict when it comes up against other adult behavioural patterns.

Other roles in adult life

As adults, there are equivalent roles to those of child, partner and parent outside the family unit. These are seen in the way we respond to other people we meet or interact with during the course of our work or spare time interests.

Subordinate role

This is a childlike role in the adult world. You are told what to do and you get on with it.

This role is not restricted simply to the work environment: it can be seen in the way any two or more people respond to one another. Some will always be led by others, whether this is in a committee or a team activity. This does not necessarily mean however that they are happy about this state of affairs. They may very much wish to play a peer group role, or even take the initiative occasionally, but the presence of a more dominant member or members prevents this from happening.

Peer group role
This is the equivalent of the partnership role in the family. There is acceptance of others in a group as being equals, with reciprocal shifts of roles between members taking place to meet different situations. This is generally a very satisfying environment for all participants.

Dominant role
Here is the parental role, benevolent or otherwise, in operation in the adult world. It may not always be welcome or appropriate.

There is the obvious work equivalent in the 'boss', but there are others outside the workplace, such as committee chairman or team captain where although leadership is required, it will may well be counter-productive if it is autocratic in nature, or does not have the approval of the whole group.

Role play
Think about the whole range of roles you play in your interaction with others during the course of an average day. You will find you adopt and shift your role play in response to the situation you are in, and to the mix of personalities around you.

One day in the life of . . .
At breakfast with your family you play two roles — that of parent and partner — at the same time.

You take your child to school and have to ask the head teacher for your child to have time off to go to the dentist. The head teacher is a brusque and difficult person who clearly regards you as an inferior. You would like to treat the matter on a peer group basis but you are forced into a subordinate role.

You return home irritated by this encounter to find the decorator who promised to come yesterday, standing apologetically on the doorstep trying to make excuses. You are not pleased. You let him know this by your tone which places you in the dominant role and pushes him very firmly into the subordinate.

Later in the day a group of friends come round to discuss a project you are all involved in. The discussion takes places at a peer group level and everyone is amicable and at ease.

You collect your child from school and take over the parental role again, adding the partnership role later over the tea table.

The phone rings. Your father would like to come and visit: he hasn't been round for ages. Don't you care about him anymore? Will you come and collect him now? — he asks. You respond in your child's role by complying with his wishes. He joins the family circle, treating you as a child. This is an uncomfortable situation: your partner is still operating at a partnership level and your child wants you to provide a parental role. You find it difficult or impossible to juggle all the roles expected of you with the frequency required by this mixed company. Your temper becomes frayed.

Supper time. You have taken your father home and discarded the childhood role. You have tucked up your own child and ceased to act the parent. Your partner has gone out to a meeting.

At long last you are able to discard all your masks and allow yourself the luxury of being yourself.

Comment

You can see from this example that while you are happy in the role you are playing, or expected to play, there is no inner conflict. Conflict sets in the moment you are pushed into a role you do not feel is appropriate at the time. This is an important point to remember when you are looking for a new career. You must not try to persuade yourself into a situation which would be stressful to you.

EVALUATING YOUR ADULT ROLES OUTSIDE THE FAMILY

How do other people treat me?

Just as the roles we are expected to play within the family unit can produce stressful situations, so can those which are expected of us in the workplace and during our spare time activities. Studying these additional roles and their effect on us is the next task.

To do this, look at the *last* job you listed in the questionnaire 'My Working History and Experiences' on page 39 in Chapter 3, and *all* the activities you listed in the questionnaire 'My Spare Time Interests Today' on page 55 of Chapter 4.

Consider both your job and spare time activities individually and think about what answers you would give to the following questions:

- Do people actively seek me out for advice or not?
- Do people listen to my opinion or ignore it?
- Do people act on my suggestions or not?
- Do people expect something from me or not?
- Do people give me responsibility or try to remove it?

Write down what you discover about the roles you played in the various situations you met in your workplace.

You are likely to find your answers will vary according to circumstances and the personalities of the people involved. Looking at your last job for instance, you will in all probability discover a broad mix of roles was expected of you, depending on what duties you were carrying out at the time — such as supervising or being supervised, giving or taking instructions, or participating in a peer group exercise as part of a team of equals.

In your social life, you are likely to find an equally diverse role play dependent on the perception of you by others in your group — as well as their individual perceptions of themselves.

When you have finished look at your answers individually. Using any adjectives you feel are appropriate, how would you describe yourself from the point of view of each of the following.

- your boss
- your colleagues
- your subordinates
- your close friends
- your acquaintances.

Do they all see you in the same light, or do different facets of your personality come into play in different circumstances? Do you influence their vision of you by a conscious change of role to fit these circumstances? Do you now believe this is a good or a bad thing? Do you feel there are some situations where you would have preferred to adopt a different role? Why was this? What was it that stopped you from doing so?

Now consider the following:

- Do I try to appear approachable or not?
- Do I enjoy being sociable or not?
- Do I encourage others to give their opinion or not?
- Do I really want other people's opinion or not?
- Do I expect things from other people or not?

- Do I prefer to act on my own or with others?
- Do I give people responsibility or try to remove it?
- Am I prepared to act on other people's suggestions or not?
- Do I give the appearance of being a caring person or not?

From your answers, how much of your true self is visible to others? Are you projecting your true image or the 'mask' you think is acceptable to them in the role you are playing? Does this 'mask' make you feel better able to cope, or does it place a strain on you?

These questions are important because if you are starting out on a new career, you might well want to discard some of the 'masks' you have worn in certain situations in the past. You may want to adopt a softer profile, or a harder one. If so, recognise the fact you actively want to change other people's perceptions of you and ask yourself how you might be able to achieve this aim.

How do I react to other people's perception of me?

How you feel about the way other people treat you can give you some idea about whether or not the role you are playing at the time is one you feel 'at home' in in those particular circumstances.

Put yourself in all the various situations you meet on a day-to-day basis. Conjure up the emotions generated by the way other people respond to you both at work and in your spare time occupations. Are there specific circumstances where you feel:

- anger
- resentment
- acceptance
- contentment
- pleasure
- satisfaction
- indifference.

Is what you feel appropriate for the situation, or not? Are you feeling satisfied because you have put someone else down unnecessarily, or because you feel you have made a positive contribution to a situation? Is the anger you feel directed at someone else or at yourself? Is your acceptance of the way others treat you due to your consenting to the status they have conferred on you, or a lack of confidence in your own abilities?

To put this into a nutshell, are you happy with the image you are projecting?

Are there any aspects I need to change?

When you are starting from scratch, you will almost certainly have to face a different set of roles from those you played in your last job.

In your new situation, you may need to retrain and accept guidance from others; you may have to listen before you can speak. In these circumstances you cannot afford to adopt the dominant role: it is misplaced and unacceptable. Instead, you must be prepared to adopt the lesser role of a willing subordinate until you have completed your training and become firmly established in your new career.

If you held a fairly senior position in your last job, perhaps where the majority of your duties and responsibilities meant you were taking the lead most of the time and directing others, you may find the mental readjustment necessary to meet your new circumstances quite daunting. Nonetheless, it is vital you recognise your changed circumstances and act accordingly. If you don't, your attitude will hinder your progress and prevent others from helping you to achieve your goal.

If you held a more humble position in your last job however, you may have a different set of hurdles to cross. Your greatest problem may be buffing up your image rather than toning it down. Perhaps you need to improve your self-confidence or assertiveness. This is especially important if you want to 'sell' your skills and experience properly to a new employer, or financial backer, or to convince a college that you have the ability and vitality to be a successful mature student.

Your self-confidence is the first thing to suffer if you have had to cope with redundancy. Even after you have completed all the exercises in this book, and come to recognise you have greater skills and abilities than you first imagined, you may still lack the confidence to sell yourself to the outside world.

If this is a major stumbling block for you, then do seriously consider joining a course at your local college or business centre to improve your assertiveness skills. There are usually several on offer, some of them probably advertised in your local paper. Check with the course provider first to see which group of people the course is aiming to attract. Many are designed to meet specific needs, such as those of women returners, or redundant executives, so make sure you choose a course which meets your own requirements. It is quite pointless putting yourself in a situation where your self-confidence could shrivel up completely because you were uncomfortable or felt out of place with the rest of the people in the group.

THE FINISHED PICTURE OF YOU

At this point, all the data gathering is complete — and so is your Self Portrait. Whether you like the picture you have painted of yourself or not, it should help you to focus more precisely on your strengths and concentrate on improving your weaknesses, if you have any.

Starting with the next chapter is the task of making sense of the data collected so far, using it as a guide to show you how to approach planning your future career path and the how to tackle the choices that have to be made.

CHECKLIST

1. What role do you play most within the family unit? Would you prefer another role?

2. What role do you or did you play most in the work environment? Would you prefer another role?

3. What role do you play most in your spare time activities? Does it differ from your main family or work roles?

4. What have you discovered about your projected image?

5. Is your projected image what you intend it to be in every circumstance? If not, why not?

6. Are you projecting an image which does not reflect your personality? If so, does this help you cope with particular circumstances or produce stress?

7. Are there any images you want to discard in your new career? If so, what are they and why do you want to discard them?

8. Are there any images you want to foster in your new career? If so, how do you think you might be able to do this?

9. How do you believe starting a new career will affect both your self-image and the image you want to project?

10. Are you anxious about adapting to new roles? If so, how do you think you might be able to overcome this?

6

Making Sense of the Data

PULLING THE STRANDS TOGETHER

The aim of this chapter is to help you with your revision, rather along the same lines as if you were about to take an examination. You have completed the coursework, now you need to brush up on the important points you have identified and bring these together into a meaningful whole.

At this stage, it is probably worth repeating what was said at the start of Chapter 1 — that to succeed in a new career you have to target your new job very precisely; you must be confident you know where you are going, and why; and that the clues to help you achieve this confidence lie in your own personal history.

Now you have a detailed study of your personal history to hand in the form of your Self Portrait, the next step is to re-read everything. There are two very good reasons for doing this. They are:

1. You need to refresh your memory, particularly if you completed the exercises in Chapters 2 — 5 over a longish period; and

2. You need to give extra thought to the points you took the trouble to identify as being especially important as you worked your way through the questionnaires, and why you felt these were significant enough to commit to paper.

There is always the temptation to rush through this procedure — DON'T. Make this a leisurely progress. Absorb everything, consider everything, particularly if you find you have written a comment which on reflection no longer seems to have much relevance, or is certainly less important to you at this stage than it was earlier. You felt it was important at the time so don't ignore it, or even worse, discard it. Try to remember what it was that made you feel you should draw attention to this point at the time: it could be very relevant.

And most important of all — try not to let your previous *type* of career, or careers, blinker your thinking. You want to free yourself from all previously conceived notions about what is right for you and start from the beginning with a clean sheet.

PERSONAL NEEDS AND SATISFACTION

A really successful career should meet your needs as an individual and give you the maximum of satisfaction in the process. To do this, it has to:

- take place in the right environment;
- reflect your true personality;
- make the optimum use of your skills and abilities; and
- reflect as far as possible your main motivational drives.

Anything less than this is unlikely to be the right sort of job for you.

What is the right working environment for me?

The most obvious clue to this question lies in the answers you gave in setting out the pros and cons of each job you did in the past (Chapter 3), and in particular which of all your previous jobs you were prepared to say you enjoyed the most.

Was this a solitary job, or were you part of a team? Were you employed by a small, medium or large scale organisation? Were you allowed to get on with the job with the minimum supervision, or were you closely monitored? Was it an indoor or outdoor job? Was it physically or mentally demanding? Was it office based or mobile? Were you expected to move from location to location as part of your career progression? Were there plenty of opportunities for training and promotion? Were your colleagues younger, older or the same age range? Were they the same sex as yourself?

From the answers you gave, you should begin to see the type of working environment you prefer and which is likely to give you the most satisfaction. If you thoroughly enjoyed working as a member of a team in a large organisation where a large proportion of your working day was mobile, be aware of this working environment preference. Keep it firmly in mind. Don't let yourself forget it.

What if I didn't like any of my previous work environments?
It is possible if you were going down the wrong road in your career that every job you did, or your entire working life ran counter to your inner self. You will know this if you had difficulty in actually choosing which of your jobs you enjoyed most. In your heart of hearts you knew you didn't like any of them.

If this is the case then look at the choice you made under the heading 'What would I like to do in future?' on page 43 in Chapter 3. Look again at what you have written in terms of the work environment you thought you might prefer. Does this still hold true now at the end of the exercise, or have you modified your ideas in any way?

If your ideas are still unfocused at this stage, don't let this bog you down. Turn to the answers you gave to 'Personal preferences in a social context' on page 56 in Chapter 4. Did you find a social pattern emerging in your choice of hobbies? What sort of environment would this constitute if transferred to the workplace? Would you be working with people of your own age? Would you be working on your own or in a group? And so on. If you still can't see your way clearly, leave the problem for a while and come back to it later. Often allowing yourself breathing space helps the thought processes.

THE PERSONALITY FACTOR

What is my true personality?

In Chapter 5 we saw how it is possible to present a whole series of different 'selves' to the outside world while our 'real self' remains hidden away. We also saw the problems that can spring from trying to act out a role which others impose on us when this runs counter to our natural inclinations.

For clues as to your true personality, ignore your work history. Concentrate instead on all the information you gathered together in response to Chapter 4. Your spare time interests are far better indicators. Remember, these are what you do because you *want* to, not because you *have* to.

Under the heading 'Reasons for doing what you do' on page 57, you should have identified the motives behind your involvement in each of your pastimes under the following headings:

- self-expression
- social contact
- helping others
- authority over others
- personal challenge
- prestige value
- individual freedom.

If one motive stood out clearly above the rest, have you recognised that this constitutes an important facet of your personality? It will therefore need to have a high profile in whatever career you decide upon.

If no clear leader emerged from your list, pay attention to those motives which still rank higher than the others. Which are they? Identify them because they each represent an important part of your personality which needs to be catered for.

What else can I discover about myself?

Look again at your pastimes. Do group activities have a large part to play? Do you hold any leadership roles, such as team captain or chairman? Are there any creative or scientific interests? Are all your pastimes solitary? Is there an element of risk involved — in the widest sense? In a nutshell, what do your hobbies say about you?

Do they tell you you are solitary or gregarious, reserved or outwardly expressive, a thinker or a doer, a leader or a follower? Do you feel this is probably a true picture of your real self? If not, why not? Remember the influence of other people discussed in Chapter 5. If you feel frustrated by the domineering personality of others in any of your pastimes, then recognise part of your personality includes a degree of lack of self-confidence, or insecurity. Don't feel overwhelmed by this knowledge: it is not an insurmountable problem and may be due entirely to very specific circumstances which would not apply in other areas of your life. It is certainly something which with the right sort of guidance can be modified or even overcome.

Look at what you have discovered about yourself and put this into a work context. If you enjoy solitary hobbies, you are hardly likely to feel at ease working as part of a team, just as if you prefer group activities, a job where you are working in isolation would be totally inappropriate. Equally frustrating would be a situation where your creative or analytical mind was thwarted by repetitive routines or haphazard working practices.

SKILLS AND ABILITIES

How can I make the best use of them?

First of all, you have to recognise what your skills and abilities are.

There are the more obvious ones which can be picked out from your educational attainments, such as literacy, numeracy or language skills. There are the additional ones which come with attaining professional or academic qualifications as well as those acquired through on-the-job training or experience. These skills can range from complex processes such as those essential to a brain surgeon, to the everyday variety such as being able to answer the telephone and communicate satisfactorily with other people.

Don't forget or undervalue the skills which do not belong to the workplace. In Chapter 4 when you were completing the questionnaire on your pastimes, you were asked to list the skills or specialist knowledge you needed in each of your hobbies or community roles. Remind yourself of these now.

Go back to Chapter 2 and your formative years. Did you develop any skills within the family which are still relevant but which you tend to take largely for granted — such as, caring for an elderly relative or handicapped sibling, coping with personal tragedy or taking responsibility at an early age?

Don't discount anything which can still be put to use, even if you really don't want to use the skill or knowledge on a day-to-day basis: it may be a useful secondary skill which is essential to achieving your main aim. You may hate driving, but if your new career is entirely dependent on your ability to be mobile, then it would obviously be foolish not to recognise the importance of being able to drive. You should be aiming to find a career which will use your best skills to their best advantage while allowing many of your lesser abilities the chance to play their part.

MATCHING CAREER TO MOTIVATIONAL DRIVES

In what way should my new career reflect these?

Go back to Chapter 4 and the 'Reasons for doing what you do' on page 57. Study the main motives you identified which lay behind your commitment to these pastimes. Your new career *must* satisfy the emotional needs these drives represent or you will never be able to put your heart and soul into the venture.

Don't delude yourself into thinking you can ignore them, especially if that is precisely what you have done in the past. If your desire for self-expression is high, then persuading yourself it is socially more acceptable or responsible to devote yourself to caring for others does nothing either for you or the people you are supposed to be helping. You have to be totally honest with yourself. Anything less will distort the picture and give you false guidelines.

In studying the motivational drives that affect your choice of pastime, you may have noticed one rather obvious omission in the list. This omission rarely applies to hobbies — unless you have included 'Investing on the Stock Market' as one of your paramount pastimes — but almost always applies to the world of work. This is:

● making money.

This drive does not necessarily play a major role, but if you need to work in order to keep both yourself and your dependants above the poverty line, it has a relevance you quite literally can't afford to ignore.

What importance do you place on making money? Has this motivational drive played a large part in your working life up until now? Do you still feel you want it to? Do you need the satisfaction of a high monetary return for what you do? Don't shunt this question into a siding. Face it and answer it honestly.

COMPARING CAREER HISTORY WITH HOBBIES

Looking for compatibility

Ideally, your working life should satisfy your needs and expectations in the same way as your pastimes do. Put in its simplest form, if there is a good match, you are likely not only to succeed, but to flourish. If there is a poor match, or even a complete mis-match, success will be achieved only at great personal cost, often resulting in the onset of stress related illnesses.

The greatest problem with a mis-match is that you can give the impression of being very successful at your job — even to yourself. You perform well because you are determined to succeed at all costs. Any inner doubts or misgivings are suppressed by your drive to take on a challenge. This situation isn't helped because you will also have the right skills to achieve this illusory success. There's nothing wrong with the skills, it's the working environment that needs changing.

Look for compatibility under the following headings:

- skills and abilities
- level of responsibility
- environment
- social mix.

Skills and abilities

Does your career history or your last full-time permanent job reflect the range of skills and abilities you know you have? Does it utilise some but not others? Which skills are under-utilised or not used at all? Are these skills 'high profile' in your non-working environment? Take note of this if they are.

Level of responsibility

Compared with your spare time occupations, how does your last work role rate? Did it involve a similar range of responsibilities, fewer or

greater? If there is an obvious disparity, do you feel this is something you
need to bear in mind?

Environment

Do your leisure activities take place in the same sort of environment as
your work, such as in an artistic or scientific, technical or theoretical
context; in large or small groups, or on your own? If the two environments do not match up, did you consciously choose these leisure activities as a positive reaction against your working environment? If this is
the case, don't ignore such an obvious move on your part to give your
personal needs a much needed outlet to express themselves.

Social mix

Do the people you choose to mix with in your spare time mirror the age
range and sex of your immediate working group? If they do not, is this
a conscious move on your part? Have you any hang-ups about working
with certain groups of people? If you have, now is the time to own up
and admit it to yourself.

RECONCILING THE FACTS

Building on what you know

At this point go back to Chapter 3 once again and what you wrote under
the heading 'What would I like to do in the future?' on page 43.

This exercise was designed to be a taster, to get you thinking not only
about what you might like to do in the future, but also in what context.

Look through what you wrote down then in the light of what you now
know about your preferred work environment, your personality, your
skills and abilities, and of course, your motivational drives. Was the
result of your brainstorming closer to the mark than you expected? If so,
you have a strong basis for being more confident about planning your
future. If not, don't give up. All is not lost.

The perfect job

Using all the information you now have about your personal preferences, your skills and abilities, write out a job description which in
your opinion would meet all your personal needs and aspirations.
Make this as broad as possible for maximum benefit. Don't forget to
include the qualities you identified in Chapter 4 on page 58. Also
include the level of financial returns if this is an important factor to be
considered.

The job to be avoided
This exercise is the exact opposite of the previous one to help you iden-tify everything you would not want to see in a job. When completing this, you must feel very strongly about what you see as the most unde-sirable elements. Use as a guideline the fact you would *never* consider taking a job or embarking on a career which had any of these facets. They must not be mild irritants which could possibly be overcome by some means or other.

The overall picture

What you have uncovered about yourself during this voyage of discov-ery might not be what you wanted to see. You may have even come to realise you are an entirely different person from the image you present to the outside world. You may have acted out this role for years and con-vinced yourself the mask you wore was the 'real' you.

You may have identified times in your life when you made the wrong choices, or had these forced on you by circumstances beyond your con-trol. You may have made career decisions on a totally wrong premise. And you may well have discovered you did not understand yourself well enough to take control of the situation sooner.

On the other hand, you may have come up with answers that seem to point in exactly the same direction as you were going before; where your life seems to have been well-planned from every point of view and your basic needs and aspirations have been largely catered for. In this case it is the small differences that have become important in your life, whether these are in the context of the work environment, the job content, or the level of responsibility. Considering what to do under these circumstances will be discussed in Chapter 7. Faced with the need to break new ground will be dealt with in Chapter 8.

CHECKLIST

1. What have you identified as being the right working environment for you?

2. What are the personal needs and aspirations you have identified which make up your personality?

3. What are your skills and abilities? Which of these do you consider to be the most important?

4. What are your motivational drives? Is there any one drive which is the clear leader and which is it?

5. Do the skills and abilities you use in your pastimes match those which you use in the workplace? If not, why not?

6. Do the roles you take on out of the workplace reflect your status within the workplace? If not, why not?

7. Do your leisure activities take place in a similar environment to your work activities? If not, why not?

8. Do you concentrate your leisure activities with the same age and sex as those of your immediate working group? If not, why not?

9. What do you see as being your perfect job?

10. What aspects of a job or career would you find impossible to accept?

7

Rethinking Your Old Career

COMING TO TERMS WITH A U-TURN

It is easy to become disheartened when situations work out differently from the way you anticipated. This is especially true if at the beginning of this book you were convinced you needed to break away from your old career, but gradually realised, as you worked your way through the process of getting to know yourself better, that you had no sound reason for making such a dramatic change. Try not to be too disappointed. In Chapter 1 it was emphasised that starting a new career was far from being an easy option. It represents a great deal of commitment and hard work and should never be underestimated.

What you are facing now is a new type of challenge — putting your old career into a new and hopefully better perspective by extracting the best parts of it and giving these a greater say in what you intend to do in the future.

IMPROVING YOUR CHANCES IN THE SAME CAREER

Your attitude to the job search

Before sitting down and scouring the situations vacant columns, remind yourself of what you want to achieve. You wanted to change your career. Now you have discovered you do not need to discard your past experience in its entirety. Instead, you need to reshape it. This is an important point, because the last thing you should do now is plunge yourself despairingly into the exact replica of your previous job. Remember, something was wrong with that job as far as you were concerned, and the exercises you worked through to build up your Self Portrait should have helped you to identify precisely what this was.

Restate your reasons for wanting to start again

Start by refreshing your memory as to the reason why you wanted to make a career change in the first place — or thought this would provide the answer to all your woes. Under the heading 'Why do I want to change my career?' on page 17 of Chapter 1, you wrote down a simple statement giving your reasons for this decision. Is this statement still valid? Have you identified any other factors since which should have been included, or which should replace the original statement now that you have had time to reflect more fully on all the circumstances? Rewrite your statement if you now feel your reasons need to be redefined.

PERSONAL FACTORS TO CONSIDER

Level of responsibility

The reshaping of many British companies brought about by economic necessity has produced 'flatter' profiles of organisational structures, with the loss of many middle-management positions. As a direct result of this, promotion prospects are likely to be affected for many years to come with employees 'locked into' the same post for longer periods than in the past. Promotion policies in the next decade will need to be developed which do not necessarily involve automatic upward movement. These may include a greater use of 'sideways' progression to broaden experience, or other measures designed to help maintain employee motivation in circumstances which they might have regarded as being career stagnation in the past.

From your own point of view, do you need more or less responsibility than you had before?

Frustration generated by being held back, or by not being given the opportunity to shine, can demoralise the best motivated of individuals. But beware of overestimating your potential. Did you fail to progress because the organisation employing you had no properly structured training or promotion policy? Were you blocked by personal animosity or indifference by your superiors? Were your abilities undervalued or unrecognised? Or had you got as far up the ladder as your abilities allowed you to go? Would your frustration have evaporated if you had been offered the opportunity to broaden your experience and skills within the existing organisational structure?

In all these discussions with yourself, it is crucial you recognise the upper limit of your own potential. If you do not, you can become an excellent example of *The Peter Principle*, where you are promoted or seek promotion beyond the point where you can work to the best of your ability.

An over-promoted individual is as unhappy as his or her underpromoted counterpart. In this case, the unhappiness stems from the struggle to maintain a satisfactory job performance in the face of potential failure.

Existing commitments

Will your personal commitments or those of your dependants have any bearing on your job search? A quick run through Chapter 2 should remind you of this if you have forgotten. Once again, remember not to underestimate these commitments, whether they are domestic, social or financial: they can affect the location and type of job you are looking for, as well as the level of responsibility that goes with it.

When you study the situations vacant pages, keep your commitments to the forefront of your mind and don't get carried away by your own misplaced enthusiasm for a job. Job advertisements can be minefields of hidden meanings. Consider the following:

.   Looking for a change of environment? Here is a challenging opportunity for a self-motivated person with a positive go-getting approach. You will be expected to maintain high standards of output in a busy work situation. Extra hours will be needed at short notice during the summer months. An excellent rewards package is available for the right person.

Who is the 'right person' this organisation looking for? Someone with plenty of vitality who is able to work under pressure; someone who can work unsupervised; someone who is prepared to put in extra hours at the drop of a hat. In other words, someone who is prepared to put their job before anything else.

You might indeed be looking for a change of environment. Also, if you are out of a job for any length of time, you can often be pressurised into seeking a 'challenging' role, into being 'self-motivated' and having a 'positive approach'. In fact, this is the standard knee-jerk response frequently expected of you by the Pick-yourself-up-and-get-on-with-Life Brigade. But can you put in the extra hours that would be required, and what level of pressure would you be working under?

What you have to be aware of is your present circumstances are unlikely to match those which existed at the time you took up your last job. This is even more the case if you worked your way up the promotional ladder within the same organisation, and did not have to face the employment market for several years. Your perception of yourself may be several years out of date and if you are not careful, you can become the equivalent of the ageing actor or actress auditioning for one of the leading roles in *Romeo and Juliet*.

The Institute of Personnel & Development (IPD) has been particularly critical of the continued use of age limits in job vacancy advertisements. In many cases there is no justifiable reason for these age restrictions — anyone of any age with the proper qualifications could easily do the job in question. In other cases however, employers are seeking the commitment level they associate with the stereotyped image of a particular age group. This stereotyping exists even when no age is actually specified in the advert, as in the example above, but it is clear from the wording used that a particular type of candidate is expected to apply.

When you apply for jobs, you need to be aware of the existence of this stereotyping and appreciate its implications. Set out below is a very rough guide to what might be expected. There are both good and bad points from the employer's point of view.

1. **If you are less than 29 years of age,** you are likely to be
   single or newly married
   ambitious to succeed
   fully mobile
   energetic and innovative
   easier to train
   more prepared to take risks
   prepared to change employers more frequently
   eager for increased status and financial reward.

2. **If you are 30-39 years of age,** you are likely to be
   married with a family
   moderately ambitious
   less mobile because of family commitments
   less energetic or innovative
   slower to train
   more concerned with financial security than taking risks
   have a greater loyalty to the organisation.

3. **If you are 40 years of age or over,** you are likely to be
   not nearly as ambitious as you were
   possibly planning for early retirement
   much less energetic or innovative
   difficult to retrain
   resistant to organisational change
   unwilling to move location
   committed to the organisation
   unlikely to be looking for another employer.

This stereotyping is quite plainly an over-simplification. It would be difficult to describe either Winston Churchill or Barbara Cartland as being 'over the hill' after they reached the age of forty. There are always exceptions. But for many of us there is a grain of truth lying behind these broad assumptions. We are not what we were ten or twenty years ago, and our needs shift and adapt to our changing circumstances.

If you want to apply for a job which is clearly labelled, or one which implies it is being aimed at applicants outside your own age band, you need to do two things.

1. Make sure you understand the assumptions which lie behind the stereotyped image of the perfect candidate and be certain you can meet the demands that will be expected of you without causing a personal crisis of some sort; and

2. Aim to overcome the in-built prejudice of stereotyping by stressing your ability to meet the challenges of the 'hidden' requirements of the job.

Financial requirements

Can you afford to do what you want to do? This is a topic which will be looked at in greater depth in Chapter 9. For now, bear in mind that no matter how determined you are to start again, you may have to modify your plans in some way to satisfy your financial needs.

OTHER FACTORS TO TAKE INTO ACCOUNT

These can include:

- change of organisation
- change of status
- change of working environment
- change of living/working location
- change of skills base.

Change of organisation

You should now know from what you have discovered about your personal preferences whether you would be happier working in a small, medium or large scale organisation. If you have been a solicitor in a large practice with specialities divided between the partners, you may prefer the smaller concern where each partner carries out a wider variety of services. If you have been working in a small engineering enterprise, you may be looking for a larger, more influential company.

Change of status

Changing your status involves a conscious decision to move up or down the ladder to meet your personal needs. It is basically about being more ambitious, or less, or ambitious in a different direction — to achieve in other areas.

This is quite distinct from a change in the level of responsibility. You can be the supervisor in charge of three or fifty employees, or a district manager in charge of three or twenty locations, but you are still a supervisor or a district manager — there is just more, or less, responsibility. Titles can often be extremely flexible in what they mean. This is very helpful in situations where you might feel some anxiety about appearing to lose face if you know you are taking a job which has an obvious drop in status.

Change of working environment

Again this should reflect your personal preferences. You can be a sales rep travelling the length and breadth of the country if meeting people is your forte and you enjoy being on the road. But you can equally well be a good salesman or woman by using telemarketing techniques if your persuasive manner is at its best over the phone and you prefer to be office based. Choose the environment that suits you best.

Case study: fighting frustration in the wrong environment

Alicia Sharp was 25. She was an only child of ambitious middle-class academic parents, sailed through school and achieved a good Honours degree in French. Her self-image was of a highly capable person who would automatically make it to the top.

Alicia joined a large retail chain as a management trainee and within three years was training graduate entrants herself. Although this was a responsible role, she realised she had been sidetracked in her ambition. Resentment set in and she set about looking for new jobs in a marketing role with large blue chip organisations. However, her applications were consistently turned down.

Alicia's problem lay in her perception of herself and the openings she had imagined would be hers by virtue of a degree. She was in fact quite average in her abilities, not particularly numerate and would have found working under pressure on financial analysis and organisational problem solving a great strain. The blue chip organisations had identified these weaknesses in their recruitment tests. Her strong points lay in her personality, her need to impress, influence and perform. Although her training post had provided her with an outlet for her talents, it had been in a completely wrong culture. She needed a status title, a colourful environment and a team of colleagues with similar personalities.

Alicia was helped to identify the right environment for her and pointed in the direction of public relations. She very swiftly became promotions and PR manager for a group of commercial radio stations.

Change of living/working location

This change could be forced on you if you are in a locality bristling with hundreds of other job seekers with precisely the same skills as yourself and a dwindling market for them. This is presuming, of course, that a market still exists for your skills in other parts of the UK. If it does not, then you are faced with the need to update your skills base to find similar employment (see below).

Relocation is a difficult option. If you are considering it, and have a family to think of, look back at all the issues raised in Chapter 2 under the heading 'Your Family Now' on page 34. If you dealt with these some time ago, make sure that none of the circumstances have changed over the passage of time and that your data is still correct. If the situation has changed and raised new issues which need to be resolved, they must be sorted out *at the earliest possible opportunity* so that everyone likely to be directly affected by a move has the chance to express their hopes or fears and feels able to support you. You must be prepared for the possibility that they may not, or that your decision has come at a crucial time in someone else's life. Resolution of these difficulties will have to come from within the family unit if you are not to create more problems than you overcome.

Change of skills base

You may say you can't teach an old dog new tricks, but if you possess skills and experience which have become outdated, you must accept the fact that unless you are willing to retrain, the chances of finding another job will become very slim indeed.

The learning curve, as it is known, may flatten out as we get older, but this does not mean that we cease to be able to learn — it might just take a little longer. If you can build on what you already know and take on the challenge of new technology — which is one of the key factors in the new industrial and commercial revolution — then you become far more employable. You are also showing a level of determination and commitment which will act in your favour with a potential future employer.

Training and Enterprise Councils or Local Enterprise Companies (in Scotland) as well as your Jobcentre, will be able to offer help and advise you on the latest local and national initiatives set up to help retrain people who need to update their skills to match current requirements of industry, business and commerce. Make use of the many and varied options open to you to enhance your chances in the employment market.

SHIFTING THE EMPHASIS

This is all about making use of your skills and experience in a slightly different way than you were using them before. It can be thought of as a half-way house between sticking with your old career and starting off on a completely new tack.

Case study: accentuating the positive

Richard Batchelor was 31. He had an undistinguished education at a good public school, failing his A-levels. Both his teachers and his family considered him to have a low capability. As a result, he was pushed into studying for a Diploma in Agriculture and Business, which nonetheless helped him secure a good job as a Farm Manager handling the large estates of a Duke. Richard however, had no interest in practical agriculture. What he was really interested in — and was good at — was running the business side of the job.

With the downturn in the fortunes of agriculture in the late 80s, the Duke decided to give up his farming operations and Richard was faced not only with redundancy but also the loss of his home.

Richard's main motivational drives were directed towards business and commerce: motivating staff, increasing production, negotiating costs and sales, combined with excellent technical management ability which much to his amazement was discovered to be of post-graduate level. He wanted to achieve, enjoyed the challenges of change, was innovative, and was a leader rather than a follower.

Richard was encouraged to see that his skills, competencies and qualities could be transferred to other commercial environments, initially within the world of agriculture. He was persuaded to pursue this course of action while considering taking an MBA Degree to confirm the evidence of his abilities.

Within six months of seeking professional vocational guidance, Richard had obtained the newly created post of Commercial Development Executive with a large European agricultural chemical organisation.

In other words, don't discard your previous experience entirely: use it in a different way, expand on it. This way you are not only carving out a better future for yourself, you have the additional satisfaction of knowing you are making the best use of the knowledge you have acquired in the past.

CHECKLIST

1. What level of responsibility will you be looking for in your next job?

2. What domestic, social and financial commitments do you have which might affect your job search?

3. Can you identify what aspects of stereotyping will help/hinder you in your job search?

4. How do you intend to overcome those which might hinder you?

5. What size of organisation do you want to work for in the future?

6. Do you intend to change your status with your next job? If so, in what direction and why?

7. What type of working environment will you be looking for in your next job?

8. Will you need to relocate? If so, what problems do you face and how do you intend to overcome these?

9. Do you need to update your skills base? If so, what action do you intend to take to do so?

10. Do you see ways in which you might transfer your existing skills and experience to other uses? If so, what openings do you think you could pursue?

8

Breaking New Ground

FACING THE CHALLENGE

Discovering there has been a mis-match between your motivational drives and your previous career is likely to produce one of two effects.

1. Relief that at last you have been able to put your finger on why you have been frustrated or bored in your last job, or unsettled at the prospect of looking for a similar type of job again; or

2. Depressed that so many years of your life have been spent apparently going in the wrong direction to no good effect.

Depression is understandable, particularly if you have been struggling against your inner self to succeed against all the odds. But don't allow this negative thinking to persist. Experience is rarely wasted, even if it has been a bad experience. Understanding why it has been a bad experience is the clue to your future success.

Case study: giving in without a fight

Thirty-two-year-old John Bailey's passion was science. His choices at A-level were a foregone conclusion, although his decision to become a vegetarian made him drop Biology for Geography. He had a very strong desire to help the environment and wanted to become an ecologist. His confidence in his mission however, was badly dented by only just scraping through his degree in Environmental Science.

Believing he was not good enough to pursue his original goal, he made no attempt to apply for scientific work and joined the ranks of the graduate unemployed, drifting into jobs for the money rather than any personal satisfaction. Seven years after graduating, he found himself as a high pressure salesman where he was not only out of his depth but working completely against his character. He felt he had wasted his life and saw nowhere to go.

John sought help from a vocational guidance adviser and discovered all his scientific, creative and practical interests were still very much alive and kicking. He was identified as a truly gifted person. Added to this, he was shown that his personality was that of a quiet introvert and thinker, in complete contrast to what he had been trying to be as a pushy salesman.

John was encouraged to see that his early choices at school had been correct; that his natural motivation, ability and disposition to be an ecologist had been right all along. The problem stemmed from the fact he had not been advised at the time that a mediocre degree did not prevent him from pursuing this goal.

Armed with a reference based on his guidance assessment, John gained a postgraduate place at Aberystwyth University to study Environmental Impact Assessment and was offered two jobs before completing his final exams, the second as a scientist for an environmental consultancy which not only matched his exact requirements, but had the added bonus of being very well paid.

RECOGNISING YOUR GOAL

At the end of Chapter 6, were you able to flesh out your original career ideas you brainstormed in Chapter 3? Do you now know precisely –

- what you want to do?
- what level you would want to work at, or aim to work at?
- what sort of working environment you would be in?
- what additional facets you would want to see in the job?

The chances are that your head is full of good ideas, but these are still largely unformed, either because you do not have sufficient information to hand on the career in question, or because you have insufficient knowledge of what possible careers might be open to you. Without this additional knowledge, you will not be able to answer the following questions –

- What retraining might be necessary?
- How long will this take?
- How will this be financed?
- What opportunities exist in this field?
- Is it likely I will have to move somewhere else to find employment?
- What are the financial rewards?

FINDING THE ANSWERS

Personal contacts
These can be your most valuable source of information. If you know anyone who is already working in the type of job you are thinking of, ask them to spare you some time to take you through all the aspects of the work involved. Press them on the pros and cons so you are certain about what you are going to be taking on.

Works of reference
Without personal contacts, you will need to turn to other sources of information.

Your local library, Jobcentre or Careers Office can help you here with reference books which you can study at your leisure. The address of your nearest Jobcentre appears under Employment Services in *The Phone Book*.

Occupations published by HMSO is available at Jobcentres. This covers around 600 jobs and has a very useful article on current occupational trends as an opener. There are details on pay, opportunities, prospects, personal characteristics needed, entry requirements, training, whether you can be a late entrant or not, and gives details of related occupations, eg actor — speech therapist, and sections on further information and reading.

If you are interested in working as a full-time paid member of a voluntary organisation, *The Voluntary Agencies Directory* has around 2,000 voluntary non-political agencies listed. This is published by the National Council for Voluntary Organisations, 26 Bedford Square, London WC1B 3HU but is available in most larger libraries.

Also useful is *The Directory of Volunteering and Employment Opportunities* by Jan Brownfoot and Frances Wilks, published by the Directory of Social Change. Around 500 voluntary organisations and charities are listed under 32 wide-ranging categories such as disability, homelessness, the arts, sport, animals, the environment, law, women, youth, religious affairs, overseas development, etc. The main contact address for each organisation, telephone and fax numbers and the name of the person to contact are listed. There is a summary of the activities covered by each organisation, and what opportunities exist for volunteering and employment as well as additional information. At the end of the directory there are also lists of further useful addresses and publications.

Second Chances is a DfEE Careers and Occupational Information Centre (COIC) guidebook for adults wanting to train, retrain or take part in educational opportunities. Target groups for the book include those seeking new careers. There is a flow-chart to follow setting out what your current circumstances are, what action you wish to take and what chapters are relevant to each course of action. There are plenty of cross references, and general information on understanding the education and training system. It also usefully includes a chapter devoted to the topic of money.

The Mature Students' Guide by Liz Maynard and Simon Pearsall, published by Trotman, is for the mature applicant wanting to get into higher education. Chapters include: what is higher education?; is higher education for you?; qualifications and preparation; choosing a course and a place to study; applying to university or college and financial support.

Springboard Job Book: the definitive careers guide is published by CRAC and is also available on CD-ROM. It includes sections putting the spotlight on a range of large scale employers; job hunting skills; career profiles and case studies; education and training opportunities and labour market information.

A very useful book if you are considering self-employment is *Self-Employment (A practical guide)* edited by Dennis Millward and published by CEPEC. There are no rose-coloured spectacles here, rather a dose of realism, plenty of advice and lots of ideas. The aim of the book is to raise issues to be faced by self-employment: the personal attributes which will make self-employment right for you; the legal issues of running a business and the need for thorough planning and research for a business to thrive. There is guidance on what steps to take before you begin trading, such as professional advice needed, thinking about communication requirements and staffing. Other sections deal with how to keep your business going, National Insurance, PAYE and VAT. There are also lists of further reading on all aspects together with suggested advisory bodies to consult.

Professional bodies

If you are aiming for a profession, you should contact the recognised professional regulating body for any relevant information. This is particularly important where examination or experience qualifications will be expected of you before you can be admitted to the profession, or where you will not be allowed to practise without being a paid-up member of the professional body.

Training providers

For non-professional training outlets, the *Yellow Pages* phone book for your area will give you a whole range of possibilities under the heading

'Training Services'. However, it is not always clear from individual entries precisely what training is on offer or who it is aimed at. You could waste a great deal of time and money in working your way methodically through the list. There is also the danger that you do not have any way of measuring the quality of the training on offer.

Your best bet is to contact your local Jobcentre in the first instance. You will be able to discuss your training needs with them and they will be able to direct you to the most appropriate training provider to suit your requirements.

Training and Enterprise Councils or Local Enterprise Companies (Scotland)

These are government funded agencies responsible for co-ordinating government training and enterprise projects in the areas they cover. They provide information on business training, youth training and adult training, and give advice on self-employment. In future there are likely to be mergers between TECs and other government initiatives such as Business Link to provide one-stop shops for such advice.

Your nearest TEC or LEC will be listed in *The Phone Book* and *The Yellow Pages*.

Training Access Points (TAPS)

Originally set up through TECs and LECs to provide up-to-date information on college courses both nationally and locally, this database is no longer available across the UK. Some TECs have opted for different software; others have set up their own databases to provide an integrated service on job openings at a local or regional level, combined with training opportunities. Some are even providing this data on regularly updated CD-ROM format to careers offices, schools, libraries, community organisations and businesses. Contact your local TEC or LEC to find out what is available in your area.

Local colleges

Contacting your local college for their latest prospectus is the easiest way of finding out what is available locally.

Distance learning

If you can't find what you want locally and know immediately your commitments will prevent you from studying away from home, the wide variety of distance learning packages now available mean you can study practically anything by fitting your study sessions into available free hours.

The Open University is the most obvious immediate choice for degree courses but there are also personal interest home study packs available. Information on courses can be obtained from

The Student Enquiry Service
The Open University
PO Box 71
Milton Keynes
MK7 6AG
Tel: (01908) 274066
Fax: (01908) 653744

Full course descriptions are available on the Internet website http://www.open.ac.uk. The addresses and telephone numbers of the Regional Centres for Wales, Scotland and Northern Ireland are on p137.

Many professional bodies have distance learning programmes for their students which you could enquire about. Correspondence colleges were the original providers of distance learning for several professional bodies and many are still providing excellent opportunities for home-based students. A list of accredited colleges and the courses they offer is available from:

The Open & Distance Learning Quality Council
27 Marylebone Road
London NW1 5JS
Tel: (0171) 935 5391
Fax: (0171) 935 2540

Although the Council is an independent body, it was set up at the request of government in 1969 to help raise standards in open and distance education and training to protect the interest of students. Accreditation includes rigorous assessment of a college's administrative and tutorial methods, educational materials and publicity. Accredited colleges are monitored and reassessed at regular intervals.

University for Industry (UfI)
This is a government initiative of the DfEE to encourage lifelong learning. At the moment it is still in its developmental stage and will not be fully operational until 2000. The concept is a public/private partnership between businesses, education and training providers, using modern technologies to make learning available at a time and place suitable for the learner. The four sectors to be targeted are retail, automotive components, environmental services and the multi-media industry. There will be a separate organisational structure for England, Scotland, Wales and Northern Ireland. Although the initiative has been given the title 'uni-

versity', the UfI will only act as a facilitator and it will not itself award or accredit qualifications.

Free confidential information and advice about learning and career opportunities are already available through the UfI freephone helpline: Learning Direct 0800 100 900. Further information on UfI proposals can be obtained from:

DfEE Publications
PO Box 5050
Sudbury
Suffolk CO10 6ZQ
Tel: (0845) 60 222 60
Fax: (0845) 60 333 60

NOT RECOGNISING YOUR GOAL

This is not an improbable situation. If you have never had any idea from an early age as to the direction you wanted to take, the mass of data you have acquired in building up your Self Portrait will have given you very detailed information about the sort of person you are, the type of working environment which would suit you best, what your skills and experience are — but no focal point in which to direct them.

If it is any comfort, there are a lot of people in the same position.

Case study: going nowhere fast

While at comprehensive school, Lynn Florence's only notion was to go to art school and become a 'colourful person'. She graduated from a London polytechnic with a degree in Fine Art and then discovered how uncolourful the reality of making a living could be. Unable to come to any definite decision, she went to Italy, taught English as a foreign language, married an Italian and lived very colourfully for eight years until her marriage broke up.

Returning to England, Lynn was alone, aged 38, without contacts and needing to support herself. She saw her only options as teaching Art or doing secretarial work. She was only able to secure part-time or temporary teaching jobs so she completed a secretarial course to bridge the gap. For the following seven years her chequered history, with no evidence of commitment, ensured she never secured a full-time job. Her 'home' life was equally unstable: she lived in a mobile home unable to break out of the vicious circle of low pay and insecurity to take control of her life and improve her prospects. She was very depressed and approaching a mid-life crisis.

Seeking vocational guidance, she was shown that although she had strong artistic interests her strength lay in her very high verbal ability. Her motivational drives reflected her early aesthetic ambitions, but also highlighted the fact that she needed a more academic analytical challenge combined with a need to help people. She had a strong caring streak, inventiveness, independence and a great deal of commitment and drive which would never have been imagined from her work history.

Lynn had started her working life with low expectations and a fear of failure and had created her own cul-de-sac by avoiding challenges. She had never used her real abilities and values. By mid-life, she felt lost and without any sense of purpose.

Lynn was shown that her artistic and sensitive traits needed to be deployed in a professional role where she could be creative and progressive; that she was a facilitator who should be in a caring role, and most important of all, that her investment in art and teaching should be used to generate new openings.

Within nine months, Lynn had obtained an Advanced Certificate in Counselling and Group work and become self-employed, finding plenty of work through the Social Services where she had previously been employed as a secretary. She also successfully completed a full-time postgraduate Diploma in Dramatherapy two years later and started her own professional practice as a dramatherapist providing services primarily for health authorities.

SEEKING PROFESSIONAL HELP

There is a great deal of professional advice available today for those seeking vocational guidance, and an increasing number of people are receiving career coaching from professional counsellors.

Skilled professionals can offer insights into your problems that friends or family can't provide. However, you must feel you are ready for career guidance to get the maximum benefit from it, and also be prepared to accept whatever it produces — both the good news and the bad.

The 'Outplacement' specialist

Outplacement firms are brought in by companies or organisations preparing to restructure themselves with the inevitable job losses that now seem to accompany this process. Reputable firms are staffed by qualified occupational psychologists and usually provide other services besides redundancy counselling, such as management development programmes, personal development and mid-career reviews. Some also provide services to individuals not sponsored by their company, but this can be expensive as fees are geared towards what an employer would be prepared to pay.

Outplacement arrived in the UK from the United States in the mid '70s as a way to help redundant executives. During the recession of the early 80s it was used to cater for the needs of more junior employees. Although outplacement services are still in the main for managerial and professional groups, there are some firms who provide guidance to other white-collar workers and also the semi-skilled manual worker.

The increased demand for their services has seen a dramatic increase in the number of firms operating in the occupational psychology field from around 10 in the early 1980s to nearly 200 by the end of the decade. Although this means a greater choice, it has also meant the emergence of 'cowboy' operators, as anyone can claim to be a careers guidance adviser.

Occupational Guidance Advisers

The British Psychological Society (BPS) keeps a list of names, addresses and telephone numbers of its qualified members who offer vocational guidance to the public at large in the various regions of the UK and Northern Ireland. Like all lists, it can soon become out of date, but a quick phone call would confirm whether or not a particular firm was still providing these services in your area. Copies of the list are available from:

The British Psychological Society
St Andrews House
48 Princess Road East
Leicester LE1 7DR
Tel: (01533) 549568
Fax: (01533) 470787

Most of the firms listed are primarily in business to provide services to companies, so do check on the level of fees before committing yourself to seeking their advice if they do offer an individual service.

One firm which specialises in individual guidance for members of the public is Career Analysts in London. This firm, with its staff of well qualified occupational psychologists, has been established since 1965 and has a high reputation for providing sound vocational counselling at a reasonable cost to people of all ages from all over the British Isles. If you want further information on the range of services available, write to:

Career Analysts
Career House
90 Gloucester Place
London W1H 4BL
Tel: (0171) 935 5452
Fax: (0171) 486 9922

Careers Service

Originally under the control of local authorities, the Careers Service now operates within the private sector with a wider remit than simply providing a link between school leavers and the world of work. Services in most areas now include help to adults as well as young people, although this is not always free because adult services are funded differently in different areas. If you want to use the Careers Service, check first whether they are likely to charge you for any advice given.

N.B. The address and phone number of your local careers service can be found in *The Phone Book*.

CHECKLIST

1. If you are clear about the career you want to follow, what do you need to know about this career which you do not know at present?

2. What sources of information will provide the answers?

3. Are there any educational or experiential requirements which must be fulfilled before you can put your ideas into practice?

4. If you need to acquire any additional qualifications, do you know what study options are available to you?

5. What is the most appropriate method of study to meet your personal requirements?

6. If you are not clear about what career you want to follow, what professional sources of help are available to you?

7. What are the financial costs of seeking professional advice?

8. Are you prepared to keep an open mind on the outcome?

9. Are you committed to acting on the advice you are given?

10. What do you understand is involved in achieving your new career?

9

Can I Afford It?

CAN I AFFORD TO TAKE THE PLUNGE?

'Affordability' in this chapter refers largely to the financial decisions facing you now you have decided what to do with your career. Whether you can afford to ignore your true motivational drives in terms of personal satisfaction has already been covered elsewhere.

It is a fact of life that whatever we decide to do, or not to do, it almost always comes down to finance. Can we afford to go on holiday? Can we afford a new car? Can we afford to re-decorate the house or to buy a new carpet? Sometimes, the choices can be more basic. Can we afford to pay the rent if we buy a joint of meat this week? Can we afford to buy the children new shoes if the gas bill comes early?

Getting into financial difficulties is a situation no one should purposely set out to achieve. Nor should you go around pretending to yourself that it really doesn't matter. It does. Being short of cash can put an unbearable strain on even the most evenly balanced of relationships. You must never allow yourself to forget this if you have dependants whose well-being is in your hands. Be positive — but realistic. Don't set out on a course of action with half-formed ideas, and the vague hope that 'something will turn up'. It might not.

Why leave discussing the financial angle until now? — you might ask — especially if it is so important. The reason is simple. Until you know precisely what your plans are going to be, you cannot work out in detail the likely expenses involved; what funding might or might not be available; what additional financial help is on offer, and so on.

YOUR FINANCIAL INVENTORY

Existing outgoings

In all probability if you have already lost your job, you will have gone through your financial position with a fine tooth comb to put your present circumstances into some sort of perspective.

- If you have not done this, now is the time to do so.

The first thing to do is to write down a list of all outstanding bills you have not paid and any credit card debts. Your immediate aim should be to pay these off *as soon as possible*, particularly the outstanding amount on credit card statements. The interest rate on these is astronomical and you do yourself no favours by ignoring them. It would also be a wise move, until you are more certain of your financial future, to stick to cash or cheque transactions and to make sure any additional cardholder keeps to the same rules. If possible, pay off any hire purchase agreements you may have, especially those where non-payment could lead to a County Court judgement against you.

Secondly, make a list of monthly outgoings *for which you have been personally responsible up until now*. A suggested list is set out on pages 98 and 99. If you have annual expenses, divide these by twelve to produce a monthly figure. Deal with your quarterly bills by adding up the last four and dividing the total by twelve. Don't cut anything out at this stage until you have the complete pattern of spending in front of you, including any house maintenance costs you may have had to fund over the last year. Even though you don't expect these to be repeated, they will provide a buffer amount in your calculations for any other unexpected items you might have to fund in future.

If a major item of family or domestic expenditure is regularly paid for by someone else, say your parents, or partner for instance, include this in a separate column, so that it does not become lost or disregarded. This is especially important if anything were to happen which meant this funding were to be discontinued, and other monies had to be found to fill the gap. Death and divorce can happen, and it is unwise to place too much reliance on funds outside your immediate control.

The Grand Total represents the amount necessary to maintain your previous standard of living.

Present income

To counterbalance the outgoings, you need to know how much is coming in from all available sources, including any entitlement you might receive or be eligible for from the Department of Social Security in the form of allowances or pensions. As with your expenditure, use the month as the base and do any calculations which are necessary for comparison purposes.

If you are receiving cash gifts from anyone as a general contribution to household expenses, make sure you note these down for the same reasons as mentioned earlier — you can't always take these gifts for granted.

Suggested headings are set out on page 101.

MONTHLY EXPENDITURE

		Personal £	Other (name) £
House	Mortgage/rent		
	Building insurance		
	Contents insurance		
	Council tax		
	Water rates		
	Electricity		
	Gas		
	Telephone		
	TV rental/licence		
	Maintenance		
	Replacements	_____	_____
		_____	_____
Housekeeping	Basic food		
	Drink		
	Cleaning		
	Laundry	_____	_____
		_____	_____
Travel	Car loan repayments		
	Tax/insurance		
	Maintenance		
	MOT		
	Petrol		
	Train fares		
	Bus fares		
	Hire charge	_____	_____
		_____	_____
Family costs	School fees etc		
	Clothing (children)		
	Partner's allowance		
	Children's pocket money		
	Outstanding loans (list)		
	. . . .		
	. . . .		
	Additional costs (state)		
	. . . .		
	. . . .	_____	_____
		_____	_____

Fig. 8. Budget for personal monthly expenditure.

Personal items	Insurance premiums	Personal £	Other (name) £
	. . . .		
	. . . .		
	. . . .		
	Subscriptions (list)		
	. . . .		
	. . . .		
	. . . .		
	Maintenance to former spouse/children		
	Savings schemes		
	Toiletries		
	Medicine		
	Dental charges		
	Clothes		
	Tobacco		
	Newspapers/magazines		
	Entertainment		
	Recreation/holiday costs		
	Birthday/Christmas expenses		
	Pocket money		
	Extras (specify)		
	. . . .		
	. . . .	_____	_____
		_____	_____

Add in 10% for cost of living increases
and unforeseen expenditure

		_____	_____
GRAND TOTAL		══════	══════

FACING A SHORTFALL

Staying in control

The worst thing you can do if your new income level does not meet your potential level of expenditure is to pretend you don't have to face the problem. You do — even in the short term. Don't let things drift until you are in too deeply to get yourself out. Get yourself back onto an even keel as soon as possible. Tell *everyone* you owe money to that you are facing financial difficulties at the moment. The economic ups and downs of this country have ensured that there are a great many schemes now available to help those who are having trouble meeting their financial obligations. You may be facing only a short-term crisis, but you can't be sure. Plan for the long-term instead.

Consider doing some, if not all of the following:

- taking steps to re-schedule any loan debt or mortgage repayments;
- informing the Council if you cannot keep up local tax payments;
- contacting the gas or electricity companies etc if you are faced with a bill you can't meet immediately;
- informing the court responsible for any maintenance order and the Child Support Agency to request adjustment of the amounts payable;
- contacting your professional body to see if there are any arrangements for deferred or reduced subscription payments. **This is vital if you are in danger of losing your professional status through non-payment.**

Trying to muddle through may only make matters worse. You want to know that you can control your finances, especially if you intend to add into the calculations the complexities and expenses of retraining or returning to study. Don't expect to have all your problems solved by other people, however. It will be up to you to show you intend to play your own part by

- cutting back on your standard of living; or
- realising some of your assets.

Cutting back on your standard of living

This is not as easy as it sounds, but it may be the simplest option open to you in the short-term.

Before you ask everyone else in the household to tighten their belts however, look at your own list of items under 'Monthly Expenditure'. Identify those items you could personally –

MONTHLY INCOME

	Personal £	Other (name) £
Wages/salary (source)		
. . . .		
Interest		
Building Society		
Bank		
National Savings		
Dividends (name)		
. . . .		
. . . .		
Fees (source)		
. . . .		
Other income in cash (name source)		
. . . .	_____	_____
	_____	_____
Dept of Employment allowances		
. . . .		
Social Security benefits		
. . . .		
Pensions (all sources)		
. . . .		
. . . .	_____	_____
	_____	_____
GRAND TOTAL	_____	_____

Fig. 9. Budget for personal monthly income.

- cut out absolutely
- cut down on a lot
- cut down on a little.

When you have trimmed your own life-style, you can perhaps expect others to show willing and follow suit.

A partner who has come to rely on you as the breadwinner may be genuinely unable to cope within the sudden reversal of fortunes. Children brought up in an atmosphere of comparative financial security don't always understand why they are suddenly unable to have what they want when they want it, or why some family activities have been drastically curtailed. An elderly relative who has been relying on you to help out financially here and there may find it difficult to come to terms with the new reality. At a time when you are under considerable stress yourself, you might find it hard to put yourself in their shoes, but you will need to. You have to remember how it felt when your life started to crumble around your ears. As far as your family is concerned, the news will have had exactly the same effect: they no longer have control over their lives, and it can be very frightening.

If you have been discussing and planning your future with your partner and dependants, you will already know the extent of their commitment to what you are trying to achieve. When it comes to financial matters, you will need their wholehearted support, particularly if you are facing a quite drastic reorganisation of your lives. Keep talking and keep calm.

Identify those areas of expenditure which have to be met to keep a roof over your heads, and everyone warm, fed and clothed. After that, it's a matter of questioning the need to continue spending under every other heading and pruning out the non-essentials.

Try to keep up the important insurance payments, for instance, but let 'the icing on the cake' policies lapse. Cut out luxury items. Choose less expensive alternatives under priority headings, provided these are just as good value for money.

Look at other areas. Do you need to use the car for instance if the tax, insurance and servicing are due? Would it be cheaper to leave it in the garage and use the money saved for public transport and taxis?

Realising your assets

This is an option which may become necessary in the longer term.

Make a list of all the items available to you which you could sell if necessary. Possible headings are set out on pages 104 and 105. Remember to deduct from the valuation any loan debts that might be outstanding. Also make a note of any variation in your outgoings which the disposal of the item would represent in your monthly expenditure. Selling a piece of jewellery might reduce your insurance premiums. Selling your home would replace monthly mortgage repayments with rental charges. Consult properly qualified professionals or experts for property and other valuables, and if you are thinking of selling the car, check with a reputable motor dealer on the current state of the second-hand car market.

Some of the items on your list will have a fluctuating value, so be prepared to revise this information at regular intervals to keep your financial picture as up-to-date as possible. It may be prudent to sell an item sooner rather than later if the market is buoyant, or defer a sale if it is in the doldrums.

It is worth remembering that household furniture, and even electrical goods, have very little second-hand value if you are making a forced sale. By the time you have taken off the cost of removal and the sale-room commission, you are likely to come away with only a few pounds in your pocket.

If you are put in the position of having to realise some of your investments, make yourself thoroughly aware of the benefit which accrues from each of them before you part with it. The question you must ask yourself must be, is the benefit a safety net for the future, or of immediate value such as those investments which provide regular income? It may be that the safety net has to be sacrificed to safeguard the present, in the hope that there will be time enough when finances improve to replace the net.

CHOICES WHEN RETHINKING AN OLD CAREER

There is a good chance that if you are intending to re-enter the job market using your old skills in a new way, once you know what way this is, you will not be out of a job too long. The situation becomes a little more difficult if you need to update your skills, and a lot more difficult if you know your job-search is going to involve looking at locations away from your present home base.

Will you need to move?
It is generally accepted that moving house is one of the top three most stressful life experiences, along with death and divorce.

It is also expensive. You have to allow for some or all of the following:

AVAILABLE ASSETS

	Valuation £	Less outstanding debt if sold £	Variation on monthly expenditure if sold £
House			
Car(s)			
. . . .			
Other properties			
. . . .			
. . . .			
Caravan/boat			
Electrical goods			
Music system			
Computer(s)			
TV(s)			
Other			
. . . .			
. . . .			
Jewellery			
. . . .			
. . . .			

Fig. 10. Inventory of assets and investments.

INVESTMENTS

	Value £	Date of maturity	Loss of monthly income if sold £
Stocks and shares			
. . . .			
. . . .			
Bank accounts			
. . . .			
. . . .			
Building Society accounts			
. . . .			
. . . .			
Premium bonds National Savings Certificates			
. . . .			
. . . .			
Other (name)			
. . . .			
. . . .			
Insurance policies (name)			
. . . .			
. . . .			
Total			

- legal fees (buying and selling)
- stamp duty
- estate agents fees
- local search charges
- removal costs
- replacement costs (carpets and curtains)
- hidden extras.

If you find yourself having to move without selling your old house, you also have to make allowances for paying two mortgages, financing a bridging loan and continuing to pay council tax on the unoccupied property, all of which are a huge drain on your resources.

Is the new area more expensive?

If you are thinking of moving to another area, get a copy of a local paper and compare house prices with the location you are already living in. Adverts by some of the larger retailers will also give you some idea as to local cost of living. Contact the local council as well and ask about the level of council tax for the area. All these costs can fluctuate widely in a relatively small geographical area.

Will you need to commute?

This may be an alternative to full scale relocation. It may be preferable if children are reaching a critical time in their education or if your partner is established in a well-paid job. The costs involved in commuting can be expensive. Don't underestimate these or the cost in terms of your personal energy level, your loss of leisure time or your availability to meet family commitments.

Will your new salary match your old?

It may not if you are consciously readjusting your status level downwards, or having to take a less responsible position until you have retrained or taken additional qualifications.

Make sure you are able to restructure your financial arrangements to take account of this, either in the short-term until you are fully qualified, or on a longer-term basis if you are not aiming for the more high-powered type of job.

Are there financial implications in retraining?

If you are required to update your skills or take additional qualifications as part of your new job, check with your employer what financial help is available from the firm to off-set any costs such as tuition fees or equipment. If you have to find the finance yourself, you need to be certain you can put the funding together. Find out too whether there are any financial or other penalties if you want to take a course which is during the working day. Your employers may expect you to update your skills in your own time at your own expense.

CHOICES WHEN STARTING FROM SCRATCH

What are the financial implications of retraining?
There will *always* be some financial outlay or pressure on existing finances if you are starting from scratch. Retraining costs money, whether you are embarking on a course of study to obtain a new qualification, or having to work out your time in a lesser role to gain the necessary experience. Affordability has a major role to play.

Affordability in this context means not only the financial implications of retraining but also the necessary input of both time and personal commitment you will need to sink into your project, and all the ramifications this can have on your own life and those around you.

Expenses involved in taking a formal course include amongst other things such items as:

● tuition fees;
● books and equipment;
● accommodation charges if you are living away from home;
● supporting the family home if you are resident on campus; and
● travelling costs.

These items alone can add up to a formidable sum, so you must be sure you can meet them as well as your existing commitments.

How can I finance my college studies?
There are many ways open to you depending on a whole range of requirements by different grant-making bodies. For instance, financial assistance may depend on –

– whether you are a full-time or part-time student;
– whether you have received grant-aid in the past;
– the level of the course you are taking;
– the college offering the course;
– the method of study you intend to adopt;
– the area of study you want to pursue;

- your age;
- a means test;

and so on. The following are just some of the avenues which might be open to you.

Maintenance costs and tuition fees

New entrants into higher education from 1999 will no longer receive grants from their Local Education Authority towards living costs. These will have to be covered by a loan. Also from 1999 students will be expected to make some contribution towards the cost of their tuition fees if they can afford to do so. Means-testing will form part of the assessment and contributions are set to a current maximum of £1,000. These arrangements are likely to change from year to year however, and will need to be looked into closely to fit your personal circumstances and the course you intend to follow.

In England and Wales you will need the latest copy of *Financial Support for Students* published free by the DfEE. Copies can be obtained by calling the information line: (0800) 731 9133, or by e-mail at: info@dfee.gov.uk or by accessing the Department's website: http://www.open.gov.uk/dfee.dfeehome.htm. Braille, audio-cassette and Welsh language versions are also available.

In Scotland you will need to apply to:
Student Awards Agency for Scotland
Gyleview House
3 Redheughs Rigg
South Gyle
Edinburgh EH12 9HH
Tel: (0131) 244 5823
Fax: (0131) 244 5887

and in Northern Ireland to:

Department of Education for Northern Ireland
Rathgael House
Balloo Road
Bangor
Co. Down BT19 7PR
Tel: (01247) 279279
Fax: (01247) 279100

Access Funds

These are limited funds distributed to colleges to provide help to students who face serious financial difficulties, or where access to higher education might be inhibited by financial problems. Details of eligibility are also set out in the DfEE booklet *Financial Support for Students*. Further information can also be obtained from the Student Support or Student Services Office of the college you hope to attend, who are also responsible for administering the fund.

Grants and sponsorships

There are several publications available to help you track down possible sources of funding.

The Grants Register
Published by Macmillan Reference Limited, this lists over 2,800 awards for students studying both in the UK and abroad.

Educational Grants Directory
Published by the Directory of Social Change.

Sponsorship for Students
Published by CRAC/Hobsons, this contains 2,500 scholarships and bursaries from 200 different organisations.

If you are studying as part of your status as a trainee with an organisation, check with the training officer what expenses are going to be paid for by the firm.

Educational Grants Advisory Service (EGAS)

This independent advice agency is for those wanting to obtain funding for further or higher education who are not eligible for statutory funding. In exceptional circumstances it can help those who are eligible for statutory funding who, after exploring all other alternative sources of funding, are still in extreme financial difficulty.

EGAS also provides detailed advice about the statutory funding system to those who are thinking about entering further or higher education. For further information telephone the information line on (0171) 249 6636.

Personal loans from banks

There are loan packages on offer from the High Street banks both for first time students and those taking further study or postgraduate courses. The packages vary considerably from bank to bank so it is worth shopping around to see what is on offer and which would suit you best.

Career Development Loans

These loans are managed by the DfEE in partnership with TECs and the high street banks, Barclays, Co-operative, Clydesdale and Royal Bank of Scotland. They are tailored to help people to pay for vocational education or training through deferred bank loans.

The loans of between £300 and £8,000 can apply to any course whether it is full-time, part-time, open or distance learning provided it is:

- vocational
- no longer than two years (although up to 24 months of a longer course may be considered.

To qualify for a loan you must be:

- over 18 years old the day the loan starts
- not in receipt of a mandatory grant or other financial support for the costs to be covered by the loan.

CDLs pay up to 80 per cent of course fees and the full cost of books, materials and other related expenses. If you have been out of work for three months or longer you may be eligible for up to 100 per cent of your course fees, as well as living expenses if your course is full-time.

During the period you are studying, and up to a month afterwards, you make no repayments and the DfEE pays the interest on the loan for you. If one month after completing your course you are registered as unemployed and claiming benefits or NI credits, you can apply to defer repayments for up to five months. At the end of your interest-free period, you start to repay the loan over the period as agreed with your bank.

Booklets giving full details of eligibility, application forms and procedural details are available from Jobcentres, TECs, careers service offices, colleges and the participating high street banks.

Full-time or part-time work

There may be no alternative open to you but to complete your studies in your own time and finance them from employment. This employment may not have any connection with what you are studying: it may simply be a means of funding your studies and keeping yourself financially secure. If you are expected to have a certain level of practical experience in your new career as well as a formal qualification, however, it would obviously make sense to obtain some form of related employment.

Savings
If the worst comes to the worst and there is absolutely no other way of funding your new start, you may have to consider digging into your savings. Obviously, you have to be absolutely sure you are not jeopardising your financial security to the point of no return by doing so.

State benefits
Social Security provision is complex and subject to rapid change. The Benefits Agency booklet FB2 *Which Benefit* gives you a broad outline of what is available, but if you want to be certain of your entitlement you would be better advised to make an appointment at your nearest Benefits Agency office and talk through your particular circumstances with a member of the Agency's staff.

Friends and relations
You may be able to turn to close friends or relatives who might be prepared to give you some financial backing. Before accepting help however, be absolutely certain you understand whether you are receiving a gift or a loan. If it is a loan, then make sure you know the basis on which it is being given. Better still, put it down in writing so that both parties agree.

What are the financial implications of needing additional experience?
Needing experience as well as being properly qualified can be an additional financial hurdle to cross. You may be able to obtain the necessary expertise as part of your course, but where this is not possible you may have to consider the following:

1. Applying for low-status or trainee posts in the first instance.
2. Taking part-time jobs in relevant fields during your vacations.
3. Taking a 'filler' full-time job and taking on voluntary work in your spare time in your new sphere of activity if this is appropriate.

Whichever avenue you take, there will be some financial impact in both the short- and long-term. Calculate what this will be and what adjustments might be necessary in your financial arrangements. Be prepared to do whatever is necessary to achieve your objective, but always bear in mind your need to maintain financial security.

Case study: discovering financial ways and means

Gill Brown was a frustrated actress working as a temporary secretary to pay the mortgage of her small London flat. She had not been successful in securing a part for a very long time and was becoming increasingly bitter. This bitterness was beginning to affect her behaviour: she was becoming more remote and very snappy with her colleagues.

Outside her work she vented her anger by joining pressure groups and campaigning for change. She composed lots of letters to influential people and began to get feedback from several sources that she was very good at this — in fact much better than many lawyers used by the campaigns in the past. This fired her imagination and she began to wonder if she could make the transition from actress to lawyer.

Gill already had a degree in English and was eligible to take a one year Law conversion course. However, she would also have to complete a further year at Bar School and then a year's pupillage as a junior barrister without any income.

She talked the problem over with her bank manager and was surprised to find the bank offered career development loans. Aged 38, she applied to law school and was given a place. The bank gave her £15,000 over two years which helped to cover her household expenses, the loan to be repaid at a low interest rate over a six year period.

Gill then won a scholarship from the Middle Temple for £8,000 as a female mature entrant. This helped to pay for the course fees and books and was not repayable. Additional small donations from charities also went towards the cost of purchasing books. By converting to vegetarian food, she was able to eat well but more cheaply, and by buying good winter clothes from charity shops, she was also able to keep down the level of her personal expenditure.

Her parents provided a financial safety net to help with emergencies and to give her a break from the very hard and intense study routine.

Gill passed all her exams and gained the 12 month pupillage with a group of barristers specialising in criminal law. Her prospects now look very good and the sacrifices she made in the past are more than compensated for by the rewards she can look forward to in the future.

CHECKLIST

1. Can you sustain your previous standard of living? If not, what areas have you identified which will need to be pruned?

2. Have you taken steps to pay off outstanding debts and informed everyone who should know of your changed financial circumstances?

3. What assets could you realise if necessary?

4. What are the financial implications of moving house? Is commuting a viable and cheaper alternative?

5. What are the short- and long-term financial implications of what you intend to do?

6. What are the costs involved in returning to study?

7. How do you propose to finance these?

8. What costs are likely to be involved in obtaining any additional experience you need for your new career?

9. How do you intend to finance these?

10. Are there other less costly or less disruptive ways to achieve your retraining objectives?

10

Stepping Out

WHAT NOW?

Not everything works out the way we expect it will. The best laid plans go awry. At the end of the last chapter, we considered the possibility of having to come to terms with being unable to reach our goal, for whatever reason.

Frustration and disappointment, even anger perhaps, will cloud your judgement if you let them. Don't. This applies whether you know right from the outset that you can't do what you most want to, or whether you meet obstacles on the way to your new career that stand between you and success. Your determination to succeed will carry you far, but it may not carry you all the way. Be prepared for setbacks along the road and try not to let them overwhelm you. Yes, it is easier said than done, but being positive can often solve seemingly insoluble problems. Be flexible in your approach, or tackle the problem in a different way.

COMING TO TERMS WITH OBSTACLES

Right from the start

If you find there is absolutely no way you can move forward either immediately or in the foreseeable future don't despair. Although you may find it difficult to convince yourself, you are now in a far better position to control your prospects than you were before you started putting together your Self Portrait. For instance, you now know your greatest strengths, your preferences, the best working environment to suit your individual personality, and which motivational drives carry you forward.

If you have no way of starting a new career, then decide how to make the best of a bad situation by *using what you know about yourself as a guideline*.

If you need to change the content of your working life — say from the indoor to the outdoor — don't push yourself back into work situations which you now know are totally unsuitable. Shift the emphasis of your old career, so that what you are looking for in a job fits your personal needs and preferences better.

If you are faced with a complete mis-match between your motivational drives and your previous career, then aim to minimise the main areas of conflict. For instance, don't apply for jobs which involve team work or high-powered activity if you are at your best working on your own or prefer the quiet, steady sort of life. Once again, shift the emphasis. Find a way round the aspects you found most irritating, or nerve-racking, by careful selection.

Most important of all, you will need to find personal fulfilment outside the working day. This means looking for the type of job which has precise conditions of employment with no commitment to put in additional hours either in the workplace itself or by taking work home. Your personal spare time is precious. You need to allow your 'real' self the chance to develop and flourish through your leisure activities.

Most jobs which are undemanding are likely to be fairly mundane, unglamorous and out of the mainstream of promotional activity. By aiming for this type of job you are making your working life a means to an end, and not an end in itself.

This situation can put you in something of a dilemma: you cannot hope to succeed at an interview if you do not show at least some basic enthusiasm for the job you have applied for. So how can you be enthusiastic about a job which is simply a means of earning a living? Precisely because it is just that: it gives you the security of providing for yourself and your dependants while at the same time giving you the freedom to develop and extend your potential away from the workplace. The content of the job, or its future potential, is not as important as the financial security and personal space it offers.

There are two other likely consequences to take into account:

1. **A potential drop in your standard of living either immediately or in the future**. Make sure your dependants understand why you have made your decision to take the slow lane. As you have probably had to give up any ideas of a new career to safeguard their financial security, your commitment to them should not be in question. If you have been talking through your ideas and including everyone in the decision-making processes, it is not unreasonable to hope that you receive their support.

2. **A happier, healthier retirement**. Too many people who make work their whole life suffer from ill-health or premature death within the first year after retirement. By making life outside the workplace the

central feature of your existence, statistically you are more likely to survive to a ripe old age with your energy and mental vigour intact. Add into this equation the increasing tendency for people to take early retirement, and you will be far better placed to make better use of your increased number of non-working years.

The short-term hiccup

Even if you can see your way to making a start on your new career, you may not be able to get off the starting blocks immediately. There are all sorts of reasons which might prevent you from putting your plans into immediate effect. You may have to wait for the beginning of a new academic year. Your finances may not be what they should be immediately but the prospects look brighter in six months' time. You may need to get some practical experience under your belt before you can apply for a particular course.

Under these circumstances, how should you tackle the gap?

Whatever you do, don't lose your initial enthusiasm for the enterprise by lack of action. If you are still employed but waiting for the beginning of a new academic year, contact the college and find out what background reading material would be useful to give you a head start. If you haven't been able to commit yourself to a course until your finances improve, do the same. Or if you need practical experience, contact someone who is actively involved in the area of work you hope to train in. Ask if they would be prepared to let you 'shadow' them during a working period if this is appropriate.

If you are out of a job, aim if you can for a 'filler' that will be useful to you in your future career, or if this is not possible, keep yourself involved in your project outside the workplace by taking on activities to bolster your enthusiasm, whether this is by reading or practical experience, by shadowing or involvement with voluntary work. Always keep your long-term aim in mind.

The long-term strategy

You may be faced with the prospect of being unable to start retraining for your new career for some time. Perhaps you will have to wait several years until the children have left school, or until the mortgage is paid for, or your partner completes a course of study. Perhaps you simply need more time to get your finances into better shape.

Sustaining enthusiasm over the long-term requires concentrated effort and a strategy designed to boost your spirits so that you never lose sight of your goal over the long interval between initial determination and putting this into effect.

Planning is the all important feature of your strategy.

- Set a specific date when you intend to make the break and start your new career.

- Set up milestones in the interval between by which time you expect to meet certain targets, such as paying off the mortgage or completing a foundation course by distance learning modules.

- Scale down your financial commitments gradually if there is going to be a strain on your budget during your retraining period.

- Revise your personal life-style over the intervening months so that you can adapt to your changed circumstances more easily when the time comes.

- If possible, join the group or body which represents people in your new sphere of work and keep abreast of developments taking place in this field.

- As with the short-term hiccup, try to obtain employment in some way connected with your new career, or arrange to shadow a potential future colleague.

- Subscribe to any publications which might provide useful information.

- Nearer the time when you intend to make the break, make a start on essential course reading.

Some parts of your plan may need to be flexible. Don't make it so rigid that any failure to meet a particular deadline becomes a crisis. Starting a new career is traumatic enough without adding unnecessary stress to the situation.

PLANNING THE JOB SEARCH

Whether you are looking for a 'filler' job, a new job in your old career, or a position in your completely new career, carry out your job search with equal care and attention to detail. You now know who you are, what you are, and what you do best under which conditions, and this gives you a head start on most candidates if you use this information properly. Don't waste this precious knowledge by sloppy job-hunting.

There is still the awful tendency if you have been under financial pressure for some time to slip back into old habits by starting to apply for anything and everything which looks vaguely hopeful.

DON'T use the scatter-gun approach to job-hunting.

DO target the most appropriate jobs and no others.

Using the scatter-gun approach

If you are going to aim at every job which you *might* be able to do then you have wasted your time completing your Self Portrait and identifying your ideal work environment. The reason you completed these exercises was to help you make better use of your opportunity to find new employment. Blasting away at anything that moves is –

– wasteful of energy and effort;
– expensive on postage and paper;
– depressing because of the high failure rate; and
– unlikely to lead to success for the right reasons.

When you apply for a job you are saying to a prospective employer — This is Me. This is what I have done. This is what I am good at. This is how I think I will be good at the job you have on offer — and you have to be convincing, not only to the prospective employer, but to yourself. When you apply for a job, you have to be certain it is *the right job for you*.

STOP AND THINK if you find yourself picking out jobs from the situations vacant columns on the basis of the 'I suppose I *might* be able to do that' theory. Yes, you might. You might even be able to convince your potential employer that you might. All you are really doing, however, is fooling yourself and everyone else.

If you manage to get a job on this basis you face three possibilities:

1. Your unsuitability for the job is spotted by your employer and you are asked to leave.

2. You discover your own shortcomings and decide you have to find alternative employment.

3. You discover your own shortcomings but struggle on miserably because you can't face the trauma of being out of work again.

None of these outcomes is desirable. They don't improve your self-image, your self-development, or your career history on future application forms.

Aiming at the most appropriate jobs
Depending on what you are looking for, there are several sources of information you can use in your job search.

Jobcentre
If you are looking for local employment in basic office work, catering, retailing, openings in the building trade and associated crafts, the Jobcentre is a good beginning.

Local papers
Again, a good source for local employment with the benefit of a wider range of job opportunities from the manual through to the manager.

National press
Advertising space in the national dailies is expensive. Firms and organisations who take space are therefore hoping to reach a wider readership and attract a good response. The ads are usually for the better paid job with attractive career prospects.

Most national dailies set aside specific days for particular career vacancies, but these do not coincide with one another and each paper operates a different approach. Some jobs appear under general listings in some papers. In others, they come under a specific category which is carried on one particular day of the week. In some cases, more senior posts belonging to the same category are published on a different day to the more junior positions. You have to keep your eyes open for the variations. And it doesn't end there. With the ebb and flow of demand in the jobs market, the national dailies vary their format over the passage of time. So you have to be clear about which papers and which editions are the most useful for you to study. Check which days are relevant for your job search to save spending money on unnecessary editions. Better still, if you are close to a library, drop in on the appropriate day and scour their copies.

Professional publications
These are an obvious choice if you have a specific profession in mind. They are often published by the nationally recognised controlling organisation or association for that profession so they also contain articles and

features which keep you up to date with the latest thinking and good practices.

Voluntary work
This is especially useful if you are aiming for a career in some sort of caring capacity. Voluntary agencies usually have excellent contacts with paid professionals through both formal and informal meetings. These offer you the opportunity to 'put yourself about', to make yourself visible to people who might have a say in recruitment, and to make enquiries about likely openings which might be available in the future. If you are seen to be doing a good job as a voluntary worker, your chances of being absorbed into the paid workforce are greatly improved.

Personal contacts
Never underestimate the value of these. You do not have to debase yourself or appear to be a 'creep' by making use of the inside information that friends or potential colleagues either offer you or are prepared to give if they are asked. Do not necessarily expect them to put in a good word for you as they may not feel this is appropriate, but they may be able to tell you about potential openings which you might not otherwise know existed, or advise you to take a particular course of action to help your application stand out above the rest.

MAKING APPLICATIONS

This is a subject in itself. If you are a bit rusty on the techniques of putting together a good application and getting the best out of job interviews, don't neglect this part of the process. It's crucial.

Regardless of what sort of job you are applying for, you could waste all your previous time and effort by sloppy or inadequate presentation. It's no good being the best person for the job if everything else about you implies that you are not.

Briefly, there are three areas you must concentrate on if you are to succeed in getting a job in a competitive job market:

1. Thorough research of both the job you are applying for and the organisation which would be employing you;

2. Proper emphasis in your application to show you can match the skills being sought; and

3.   Effective personal presentation at all points of contact with your potential employer, whether this is in the written form, on the phone, or at an interview.

Researching the job and organisation

Employers are looking for someone who not only fits the bill as far as the job is concerned, but also someone who is interested in the organisation. This is especially true in larger concerns and those with a good career structure. But even small-scale firms often want to see potential employees being interested in working for them rather than their competitors.

An applicant who gives the impression he or she has weighed up the alternatives and decided to apply for a position with a particular firm is giving the strongest signal of all — I like you. It is a natural reaction in everyone to like other people who like us — and recruiters are no different in this respect.

Effective personal presentation

In writing

It should go without saying that anything written to your potential future employer should be legible, coherent and well set out. This applies to letters, application forms or your curriculum vitae.

They should be informative, concise and precise. Anything more will be a turn-off, particularly to a busy personnel officer who might be sifting through hundreds of similar applications.

If your standard of handwriting is poor, then arrange for written work to be typed. Beware of printed application forms which do not conform to standard typing spaces. The effect of a badly typed form is as negative as a badly written one. In these circumstances, you are better advised to develop your own style of clear printing for use on application forms only.

On the phone

Before you make contact, know who you want to speak to and be prepared to be referred to someone else if your initial point of contact is not available. Know what you want to say — and say it — nothing else. Make sure if someone takes a message that you give them all the information necessary to pass on the correct information.

Just like your written work, your phone calls should be informative, concise and precise.

At interview

If you have not had the experience of an interview for some time, brush up on your technique. It could let you down. This applies too if you have had several interviews but no successes to date. Your presentation might be what's at fault, not your qualifications to do a good job.

There are a whole range of books available both at booksellers and libraries to help you improve your interview performance. Before choosing which one is right for you however, check whether it is written for the UK or the US market. US interviewing techniques are substantially different from those adopted by most recruiters in the UK. Unless you intend to work for a US firm, the advice offered by these books is likely to give you a distorted view of what to expect from an interview, and encourage you in adopting the sort of approach which would not necessarily meet with universal approval here.

SPECIAL PROBLEMS FOR CAREER CHANGERS

Persuading potential employers or financial backers to take you seriously

If you are branching out into an entirely new field, your main problem is to convince other people who need to be convinced that you aren't just taking a leap into the dark. To do this, your application, whether this is for a job or financial backing, *must* bring out the following points:

- your transferable skills;
- your willingness to train or retrain;
- any evidence of preliminary training already undertaken;
- any evidence of leisure activities which support your decision to change careers;
- any evidence of current experience, such as voluntary work, shadowing or temporary employment in a similar or related field, which supports your application;
- any professional references to back up your decision to take a new career direction; and
- anything else which might add credence to your decision.

Pitfalls to avoid

Dwelling on the past

The major problem you have to overcome is the tendency to concentrate on your previous misfortune. This is very easily done if you have had to struggle to readjust your life or make the best of a bad job in coming to terms with your future.

Applications riddled with negative words and phrases such as 'unfortunately'. 'I was unable to . . .'. 'I failed . . .' and the like are an immediate turn off. Avoid them like the plague. Applications must be positive and optimistic — but not over-optimistic. Choose your words carefully, reread what you have written and ask yourself what impression you are giving.

The all-purpose curriculum vitae
It is tempting to draw up your CV, run off a string of photocopies and use it rather like a standard letter whenever a CV is requested. This is fine if you are aiming at a broad range of similar jobs. If you are targeting a specific post however, an all-purpose CV is less likely to bring out the qualities you want to emphasise the most. This is especially true when you are changing careers.

An explanatory covering letter might serve to clarify matters, but you are gambling on the willingness of a busy personnel officer to study additional material, the possibility of your explanation being overlooked, or the potential for the letter to become separated from your CV and be lost.

It may take longer to prepare, but you would be better advised to shape your CV to match the requirements of each particular job. Keep it to a single sheet of A4 and reduce your covering letter to the basic point of telling the reader which job you are applying for. Once your application is in the correct pile, it no longer matters if the covering letter becomes detached.

If you are unsure of how to produce a good CV, borrow or buy a book on the subject and learn how to present yourself to the best of your ability in as concise and attractive a manner as possible.

Remember, you owe it both to yourself and to those who depend on you to succeed in your new career. More and more people are doing just that.

CHECKLIST

1. If you are faced with being unable to make a change in your career, what plans have you made to continue your self-development away from the workplace?

2. If you are unable to start on your new career immediately, what strategies do you intend to adopt to keep your enthusiasm alive in the short-term?

3. If you are having to accept it will be some time before you can start your new career, what is your long-term strategy to help you achieve your goal?

4. What events could alter the timescale of your strategy and in what way?

5. What sources of information have you identified as being the best ones for the type of job you are looking for?

6. What selection criteria are you adopting when studying job vacancy notices? Are these appropriate to your needs?

7. What sources of information are available to you to carry out background research into the job on offer and the organisation offering it?

8. What areas of your personal presentation do you feel you need to brush up on and how do you intend to do this?

9. What aspects of your experience, skills or ability do you feel it is important to stress in your job application?

10. What aspects, if any, of your career history do you feel should play a less important role?

Appendix 1:
Personal Milestones

Part 1 – Data Gathering	**Relevant Dates**	
	Completed	*Revised*
1 Review of why you want to change your career.	_____	_____
2 Research of job market and employment trends.	_____	_____
3 Completion of family background questionnaire.	_____	_____
4 Completion of personal details questionnaire.	_____	_____
5 Review of family influences/ traumas/ experiences.	_____	_____
6 Completion of education, training and achievements questionnaire.	_____	_____
7 Review of educational influences/achievements.	_____	_____
8 Completion of present family questionnaire.	_____	_____
9 Completion of working history and experience questionnaire.	_____	_____
10 Review of your first full-time employment.	_____	_____
11 Review of subsequent jobs.	_____	_____
12 Identification of what you liked most/least about a job.	_____	_____

		Relevant Dates	
		Completed	*Revised*
13	Identification of which job you enjoyed most and why.	_____	_____
14	Brainstorming what you would like to do.	_____	_____
15	Identification of possible career openings based on 14.	_____	_____
16	Identification of what might be stopping you from doing these.	_____	_____
17	Identification of ways in which any hurdles might be overcome.	_____	_____
18	Completion of hobbies and interests questionnaire.	_____	_____
19	Compilation of a list of personal initiatives.	_____	_____
20	Completion of your present interests questionnaire.	_____	_____
21	Review of the social context of your hobbies and interests.	_____	_____
22	Identification of your favourite spare time interest.	_____	_____
23	Review of the motivational drives behind your spare time interests.	_____	_____
24	Translation of these motivational drives into desirable qualities in the workplace.	_____	_____
25	Completion of fictitious job advertisement seeking these qualities.	_____	_____
26	Review of your various life roles within the family.	_____	_____
27	Review of roles in the working environment.	_____	_____

	Relevant	**Dates**
	Completed	*Revised*

28 Review of roles in the non-working environment.   _____   _____

29 Review of your self-image.   _____   _____

30 Identification of any aspects of your image you would want to change.   _____   _____

Part II – Using the Data

31 Identification of the right working environment for you.   _____   _____

32 Review of the effect of the influence of your personality factors and motivational drives on your choice of future career.   _____   _____

33 Identification of the full range of your skills and abilities.   _____   _____

34 Identification of the preferred level of responsibility in your work environment.   _____   _____

35 Identification of the preferred social mix in your work environment.   _____   _____

36 Completion of the job description of your 'perfect' job.   _____   _____

37 Identification of the type of job you want to avoid.   _____   _____

Part III – Rethinking the Old Career

38 Review and restatement of why you want to change your career.   _____   _____

39 Review of preferred level of responsibility.   _____   _____

40 Review of existing commitments.   _____   _____

41 Identification of which stereotype matches your present circumstances.   _____   _____

		Relevant	**Dates**
		Completed	*Revised*

42   Identification of preferred size of organisation in the work environment.   _____   _____

43   Identification of any preferred change of status in the work environment.   _____   _____

44   Identification of preferred working environment.   _____   _____

45   Review of possible work locations outside your immediate area.   _____   _____

46   Review of skills base.   _____   _____

47   Identification of any retraining requirements.   _____   _____

Part IV – Breaking New Ground

48   Identification of what you want to do.   _____   _____

49   Identification of what level you want to aim for.   _____   _____

50   Identification of preferred working environment.   _____   _____

51   Identification of any additional facets you want to see in your new job.   _____   _____

52   Identification of what retraining is needed.   _____   _____

53   Review of methods and financing of any essential retraining.   _____   _____

54   Identification of job opportunities in your chosen field.   _____   _____

Part V – Finance

55   Completion of your monthly expenditure questionnaire.   _____   _____

	Relevant Dates	
	Completed	*Revised*

56 Completion of your monthly income
    questionnaire. _____ _____

57 Review of your financial situation. _____ _____

58 Completion of your available assets
    questionnaire. _____ _____

59 Completion of your investments
    questionnaire. _____ _____

60 Identification of costs involved in relocating. _____ _____

61 Identification of financial implications of
    retraining. _____ _____

62 Identification of sources of additional
    funding. _____ _____

Part VI – Planning the Future

63 Completion of short-term strategy. _____ _____

64 Completion of longer-term strategy. _____ _____

65 Completion of application to college. _____ _____

66 Identification of appropriate 'filler' jobs. _____ _____

67 Preparation of appropriate CV. _____ _____

68 Review of personal presentation in a job
    hunting situation. _____ _____

69 Identification of any areas needing
    improvement. _____ _____

70 Identification of time-scale when data will
    need to be reviewed. _____ _____

Appendix 2
Personal Telephone Directory

Description	Contact Name	Number
Jobcentre	....	....
Library	....	....
Local Education Authority	....	....
Careers Office	....	....
Training Agency	....	....
Local TEC (or LEC)	....	....
College or University	....	....
Student Support or Student Services Office	....	....
National Office of Professional Association or Body	....	....
Local Office of Professional Association or Body	....	....
Careers Guidance Specialist	....	....
Bank	....	....
Benefits Agency	....	....
Other	....	....
....	....	....
....	....	....
....	....	....

Appendix 3
Additional Case Studies:
Turning Hobbies into Careers

Catherine Gray (28) – Single

Catherine had always been interested in the Arts and her hobbies included collecting antiques and restoration. She took a Diploma in Secretarial Duties and the Liberal Arts but was unable to focus on which career to follow. Eventually, she took up employment in an estate agency.

Feeling she had made the wrong choice she consulted an occupational psychologist. Her assessment tests confirmed that her strongest interests lay in the Arts and it was suggested she should take a course in the Applied Arts and Interior Design.

More confident in her approach, Catherine followed up the suggestion and completed a course in the History of Art, gaining employment with one of the larger auction houses as well as doing research for the Victorian Picture Department with the ultimate goal of becoming an expert.

Mary Bullen (32) — Single

Mary had a variety of hobbies, but her main interests lay in cookery and nutrition. She had completed a languages degree at university and then a course for the bi-lingual secretary. Her working record however was symptomatic of having made the wrong choice at university. Her jobs included a succession of short-term commitments as secretary, courier and waitress, amongst others.

Career guidance highlighted Mary's desire to escape from a desk-bound job and to maximise the interest she had in cookery. She was advised to take a good quality cookery course with the aim of running her own restaurant at some stage in the future. Mary followed up the advice and completed a Diploma in Vegetarian Cookery and subsequently gained employment as a chef.

Ann Stuart (18) — Single

Ann had completed her A-Levels and was about to start a Foundation Course at Art School when she lost confidence in what she was doing. Her main spare time interest was voluntary work on a playscheme with handicapped children and she was beginning to think she should be considering a more care orientated career.

Her career counsellor was able to suggest the amalgamation of both interests by following up the Foundation Course with a Fine Arts Degree and then a postgraduate course in Primary School Teaching and Art Therapy. Ann embarked on this course of action whilst still keeping in touch with her voluntary work and was able to feel far more confident about her future.

Diane Matthews (29) — Married

Diane's parents were both very academically inclined and encouraged her to follow in their footsteps. Diane was equally as gifted and eventually she obtained a PhD in Biochemistry going on to become a research scientist herself.

Diane's hobbies however were in stark contrast to the 'blue-stocking' image of her profession. She loved sports and was particulary keen on hot-air ballooning which she was very good at. Gradually, she began to realise that the life of a research scientist was not for her.

Career guidance highlighted the mis-match between Diane's work environment and her true motivational drives and interests. It was suggested that she should consider taking a business qualification with a view to moving eventually into the recreation and leisure field.

Having accrued a reasonable savings buffer during her working life, Diane decided to take the plunge and planned to resign her post and become a professional balloonist straightaway.

Jane Woodville (31) — Divorced

Jane's interests included dance, travelling, herb-collecting and gardening. She had taken a Bi-lingual Secretarial Diploma and then Teaching English as a Foreign Language and subsequently got a job as a secretary in the oil industry. However, she disliked being unable to control her own working day and became increasingly frustrated. The break-down in her marriage only made matters worse.

Jane's assessment tests highlighted her need to be self-employed and the strong interest she had in alternative health regimes. She was advised to consider using these strengths to strike out on her own. After taking various suggested courses, she was able to set up a massage and healing practice aimed at stress-reduction through holistic therapy.

Anne Robson (22) — Single

Anne really had no idea what career she should follow. She took one year of a Diploma in Social Science and dropped out, only to find herself unemployed and directionless.

Anne's hobbies were very much centred on the performing arts: dancing, acrobatics, singing and acting, but she never believed she could make a career out of pursuing them. Based on her assessment tests, her careers adviser suggested she should take these interests far more seriously, particularly in the spheres of dance and movement. Anne took the advice, joined a Circus School and having secured jobs in touring companies was able to finally form her own group and tour abroad.

Glossary

Access Funds: government money given to colleges to help students in financial difficulties.

Benefits Agency: the section of the Department of Social Security which deals with the assessment, allocation and distribution of state benefits.

British Psychological Society (BPS): the professional body for practising psychologists in Great Britain.

career guidance: see vocational guidance.

Career Development Loans (CDLs): funds managed by the Employment Department in partnership with a number of high street banks available to support a wide range of vocational courses.

Careers Service: previously a local authority department primarily interested in helping young people find employment, now part of the private sector providing a broader range of services to potential employees of all age-groups as well as assisting employers in recruitment needs.

curriculum vitae (CV): a resumé of personal details, interests and previous employment often requested *in lieu of* of an application form.

DfEE: the central government Department for Education and Employment set up to provide an integrated approach to education and employment matters.

Disability Discrimination Act 1995 (DDA): an Act to prevent employers of 15 or more people from treating a disabled person less favourably than an able-bodied person unless there is a very good reason for doing so. Disability under the Act includes physical, sensory or mental disability as well as severe disfigurement.

distance learning: a variety of study methods which do not involve regular attendance at college.

employment tribunal: a quasi-judicial body set up to resolve employment rights disputes (previously known as an industrial tribunal).

Institute of Personnel and Development: the professional body for personnel and training officers in the UK and the Republic of Ireland.

Jobcentre: part of the Employment Service of the Department for

Education and Employment (DfEE) providing advice and guidance on jobs and an advertising service for job vacancies.

learning curve: the line on a graph depicting the ability to learn in relation to age.

life skills: practical and social skills which contribute towards getting the best out of life.

means-testing: the calculation of the amount of assistance to be given or contribution made taking into account personal or family income offset by specific allowances.

motivational drives: aspects of personality which decide priorities in the desire to do one thing rather than another.

occupational psychologist: a trained practitioner in human behaviour who can advise on the best career to match individual skills, personality and motivational drives.

outplacement: an imported term from the USA meaning redundancy, usually involving active counselling by a firm of occupational psychologists.

The Peter Principle: the hypothesis that people are promoted to the job immediately above their level of competency.

portable skills: special talents or abilities which can be adapted or reshaped by an individual to suit different working environments.

proactive: taking the initiative rather than waiting for events to happen.

reactive: responding to events rather than taking the initiative.

redundancy: the loss of a job when this is no longer required by the employing company or organisation.

Training and Enterprise Councils (TECS) or Local Enterprise Companies LECS (in Scotland): government funded agencies run by local industrialists and other employers responsible for coordinating government training and enterprise projects in their areas.

transferable skills: see **portable skills.**

tuition fees: the sum which a college or university charges to help meet the cost of teaching students on a course.

University for Industry (UfI): a government initiative to improve the skills and capabilities of everyone who is in work or hopes to join the workforce.

vocational guidance: professional advice on the most appropriate work to match personal qualities and skills.

Useful Addresses

The British Psychological Society
    St Andrews House
    48 Princess Road East
    Leicester
    LE1 7DR
    Tel: (0116) 254 9568
    Fax: (0116) 247 0787

Career Analysts
    Career House
    90 Gloucester Place
    London W1H 4BL
    Tel: (0171) 935 5452
    Fax: (0171) 486 9922

Trotman & Company Ltd
    12 Hill Rise
    Richmond
    Surrey
    TW10 6AU
    Tel: (0181) 332 2132
    Fax: (0181) 332 0860

The Open & Distance Learning Quality Council
    27 Marylebone Road
    London NW1 5JS
    Tel: (0171) 935 5391

Department for Education and Employment Publications
    PO Box 5050
    Sudbury
    Suffolk CO10 6ZQ
    Tel: (0845) 609 9960

Scottish Office Education Department
   Gyleview House
   3 Redheughs Rigg
   South Gyle
   Edinburgh
   EH12 9HH
   Tel: (0131) 244 5823
   Fax: (0131) 244 5887

Department of Education for Northern Ireland
   Rathgael House
   Balloo Road
   Bangor
   Co. Down BT19 7PR
   Tel: (01247) 279279
   Fax: (01247) 279100

The Open University
   PO Box 71
   Milton Keynes MK7 6AG
   Tel: (01908) 274066
   Fax: (01908) 653744

The Open University in Wales
   24 Cathedral Road
   Cardiff CF1 9SA
   Tel: (01222) 665636
   Fax: (01222) 227930
   E-mail: R10@open.ac.uk

The Open University in Scotland
   10 Drumsheugh Gardens
   Edinburgh EH3 7QJ
   Tel: (0131) 225 2889
   Fax: (0131) 220 6730
   E-mail: R11@open.ac.uk

The Open University in Northern Ireland
   40 University Road
   Belfast BT7 1SU
   Tel: (01232) 323722
   Fax: (01232) 230565
   E-mail: R12@open.ac.uk

Further Reading

An A-Z of Careers and Jobs, Diane Burston (Kogan Page, 8th edition)
Applying for a Job, Judith Johnstone (How To Books)
The Book of Career Questions, Max Eggert (Trotman)
Build Your Own Rainbow, Barrie Hopson and Mike Scally (Management Books 2000)
Career Change, Ruth Lancashire and Roger Holdsworth (Hobsons)
Career Planning for Women, Laurel Alexander (How To Books)
Careers Encyclopedia, Audrey Segal (Cassell, 14th edition)
A Careers Guide for Adults, Margaret Korving (Trotman)
Doing Voluntary Work Abroad, Mark Hempshell (How To Books)
Finding a Job with a Future, Laurel Alexander (How To Books)
Getting the Right Job, Judy Skeats (Ward Lock)
How to Work from Home, Ian Phillipson (How To Books)
Independent Careers, edited by Klaus Boehm and Jenny Lees-Spalding (Bloomsbury)
Know Your Own Personality, Glen Wilson and H. J. Eysenck (Penguin)
Manage Your Own Career, Ben Ball (British Psychological Society & Kogan Page)
Managing Your Personal Finances, John Claxton (How To Books)
The Mid Career Action Guide, Derek and Fred Kemp (Kogan Page)
Offbeat Careers; Sixty ways to avoid becoming an accountant, Vivien Donald (Kogan Page)
Passing That Interview, Judith Johnstone (How To Books)
Penguin Careers Guide, Anna Alston and Anne Daniel (Penguin, 10th edition)
Surviving Redundancy, Laurel Alexander (How To Books)

Index

APPLYING FOR A JOB
How to sell your skills and experience to a prospective employer

Judith Johnstone

Tough new realities have hit the jobs market. It is no longer enough to send employers mass-produced letters and CVs with vague details of 'hobbies and interests'. Employers want to know: 'What skills have you got? How much personal commitment? Will it be worth training you in the longer term?' This book shows you step-by-step how to tackle job applications, how to decide what you are really offering, and how to sell this effectively to your future employer. 'Very practical and informative.' *Phoenix* (Association of Graduate Careers Advisory Services). Judith Johnstone is a qualified local government administrator and Member of the Institute of Personnel & Development.

160pp illus. 1 85703 245 4. 4th edition.

FINDING A JOB WITH A FUTURE
How to identify and work in growth industries and services

Laurel Alexander

If you want to ensure a long lasting career move in the right direction, you need to read this book which sets out in a practical way, growth areas of industry and commerce. Discover the work cycle of the future based on job specific skills, abstract skills, continuous learning and life-time career planning. Learn about flexible ways of working. Laurel Alexander is a manager/trainer in career development who has helped many individuals succeed in changing their work direction.

144pp illus. 1 85703 310 8.

SURVIVING REDUNDANCY
How to take charge of yourself and your future

Laurel Alexander

This book sets out in a helpful way how to survive the first few weeks of redundancy, both practically and emotionally. It explains how to redefine your work motivations, how to create a professional jobsearch strategy and network your skills, how to approach self-employment, contract and temporary work as well as educational and training options. Laurel Alexander has helped many individuals succeed in changing their career direction.

156pp illus. 1 85703 187 3.

PASSING THAT INTERVIEW
Your step-by-step guide to achieving success

Judith Johnstone

Using a systematic and practical approach, this book takes you step-by-step through the essential pre-interview groundwork, the interview encounter itself, and what you can learn from the experience. The book contains sample pre- and post-interview correspondence, and is complete with a guide to further reading, glossary of terms, and index. 'This is from the first class How To Books stable.' *Escape Committee Newsletter*. 'Offers a fresh approach to a well documented subject.' *Newscheck* (Careers Service Bulletin). 'A complete step-by-step guide.' *The Association of Business Executives*. Judith Johnstone is a Member of the Institute of Personnel & Development; she has been an instructor in Business Studies and adult literacy tutor, and has long experience of helping people at work.

144pp illus. 1 85703 360 4. 4th edition.

WRITING A CV THAT WORKS
Developing and using your key marketing tool

Paul McGee

What makes a CV stand out from the crowd? How can you present yourself in the most successful way? This practical book shows you how to develop different versions of your CV for every situation. Reveal your hidden skills, identify your achievements and learn how to communicate these successfully. Different styles and uses for a CV are examined, as you discover the true importance of your most powerful marketing tool. Paul McGee is a freelance Trainer and Consultant for one of Britain's largest outplacement organisations. He conducts marketing workshops for people from all walks of life.

128pp illus. 1 85703 365 5. 2nd edition.

GETTING THAT JOB
The complete job finders handbook

Joan Fletcher

Now in its fourth edition this popular book provides a clear step-by-step guide to identifying job opportunities, writing successful application letters, preparing for interviews and being selected. 'A valuable book.' *Teachers Weekly*. 'Cheerful and appropriate . . . particularly helpful in providing checklists designed to bring system to searching for a job. This relaxed, friendly and very helpful little book could bring lasting benefit.' *Times Educational Supplement.* 'Clear and concise . . . should be mandatory reading by all trainees.' *Comlon Magazine* (LCCI). Joan Fletcher is an experienced Manager and Student Counsellor.

112pp illus. 1 85703 380 9. 4th edition.

STAYING AHEAD AT WORK
How to develop a winning portfolio of work skills and attitudes

Karen Mannering

The world of work is changing and employers are demanding more than just qualifications. To stay employed it is vital that you build a flexible portfolio of skills that say more about how you work and interact with others, than just the job you do. Getting ahead is tough, staying ahead can be tougher still. This book includes techniques to help you develop that 'something special' that will give you the edge over colleagues. You will also learn how to develop transportable soft skills that will ensure your future employability. Karen Mannering has worked extensively in the field of personal development, helping people build up a portfolio of skills that will enhance their professional careers.

144pp illus. 1 85703 298 5.

PREPARING A BUSINESS PLAN
How to lay the right foundations for business success

Matthew Record

A business plan is the most important commercial document you will ever have to produce, whether you are just starting out in business, or are already trading. A well thought out and carefully structured plan will be crucial to the survival and long-term success of the enterprise. Poor planning has been identified as the major cause of business failure. With the odds so stacked against success, make sure YOUR business gets off to the right start. Matthew Record is a business consultant specialising in the preparation of business plans for a variety of commercial clients. His company, Phoenix Business Plans, is based in Dorset.

158pp illus. 1 85703 374 4. 2nd edition.